To Professor Sara Lee, pioneering Jewish educator

— J.B.K. and J.D.S.

CONTENTS

Why Study Jewish History?

Is Judaism a national identity, like being American? An ethnic identity, like being an Italian-American? A religion, like being Christian? Why is Hebrew the language of the Jews? And why is Israel our homeland?

To answer these questions, imagine a time when *all* Jews lived in a country of our own. Just as Italians live in Italy, Mexicans in Mexico, and Swedes in Sweden, so, too, our ancestors, the Israelites, lived in Israel. It was more than twenty-five hundred years ago. We spoke Hebrew, were loyal to our king, worshipped as the majority of citizens did, and served in our army—the armed forces of ancient Israel.

Jews now live in countries around the globe. The majority of Scottish Jews live in Edinburgh and Glasgow, the two largest cities in the country.

Back then there were thousands of Jews. Today there are millions. So how did the Jews grow from a tiny nation to an international community? Why did so many leave Israel? Where did they go? And what do we have in common with our ancestors and with Jews who now live as far away as Greece, India, and Iran?

As you read *The History of the Jewish People*, you will discover that our history is the story of a determined people. In every century, we have adapted to changing times with creativity and a sense of purpose while holding fast to our core beliefs. Our courage and determination have been rewarded by each generation's enriching contributions to Jewish tradition.

In addition, you will discover that you are not just *studying* our people's extraordinary journey—you are also *part of the action*. You will consider how your life compares to the lives of those who came before you and how their decisions influence yours. Most important, you will discover that Jewish history is a story that begins thousands of years ago, moves across and around the world, and leads up to your community, your family, and you. By studying our history you can stand on the shoulders of those who came before you, view the past and learn from it, then turn toward the future to help build a better, stronger world.

How Do We Do It?

Over the centuries, the Jewish people have faced many challenges. They include being cast out from our native land and spread out around the world, often suffering the hardships of poverty and oppression. Yet our people survive.

How do we do it?

Some think we continue to survive because of our belief in God and the teachings of the Bible. Our faith and tradition have given us the wisdom and strength to overcome difficult times and live with joy and courage.

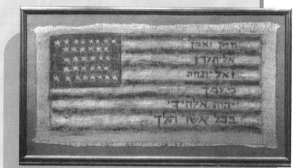

The Hebrew verse on this Union flag may have comforted Jewish soldiers during the American Civil War: "Be strong and have courage; do not be terrified or anxious, for Adonai, your God, is with you wherever you go" (Joshua 1:9).

Some think it is our sense of purpose that preserves us. Jewish tradition teaches that we have an important role to fulfill, that it is our duty to help bring justice and goodness into the world. This sense of purpose inspires us to maintain our identity and our values.

What do you think?

Amazingly, we have not only survived, we have also flourished. And we have enriched the world, beginning with our Torah, and including contributions to science, art, medicine, and peace. These accomplishments account for 20 percent of the Nobel Prizes awarded since 1901. What a feat for a people who make up only .2 percent of the world's population!

Again, how do we do it?

Some think it is our questioning nature. The prophets taught us to question the way we live—are our actions generous or selfish, truthful or dishonest, just or unjust? Perhaps questioning helps us identify both problems and opportunities that are not always obvious.

As you read *The History of the Jewish People,* consider what helped our people succeed in the larger world, even as we maintained our Jewish identities. You may discover more than one answer, each of which enriches your life.

The Four Questions are a highlight of the seder. They remind us to think about why and how we celebrate Passover. How has asking questions and searching for answers helped you learn and solve problems?

Introduction
The Birth of Our People and Monotheism

Abraham and Sarah were the first Jews. The Bible tells us that they left their home and all they were familiar with to go to the Land of Canaan. How do you think they felt on their journey? Why do you think so?

As Numerous as the Stars

Where does our story begin? The Bible teaches that it starts with our patriarch Abraham. The Book of Genesis tells us that God commanded Abraham: "Go forth from your land," to the Land of Canaan, which is what Israel was called in ancient times. It also teaches that God made a covenant, or agreement, with Abraham. According to the covenant, Abraham's descendants, the Israelites, would become as numerous as the stars and would inherit the Land of Canaan.

The Israelites gradually settled in Canaan between 1200 and 1050 BCE. Most of them were farmers and sheep and cattle herders. The Torah describes Canaan as "a land of wheat and

Learning Your BCEs

We use BCE (before the common era) and CE (common era) instead of BC and AD, which are Christian classifications. BCE and CE refer to the same years as BC and AD.

History or Religious Teachings?

The Bible contains stories about the beginnings of the Jewish people, but its greatest value is as a sacred text—a book of stories and religious laws and instructions. Among its many teachings are moral lessons that are accepted by all peoples, for example, the commandments against murder and stealing. Other teachings, such as the commandments to observe Shabbat and study Torah, are meant specifically for the Jewish people.

As you learn more about Jewish history, you may note differences between historical and biblical accounts. Remember that each presents a different type of knowledge. Historians try to uncover the literal facts of Jewish history. The Bible teaches the spiritual values of the Jewish people, such as the importance of pursuing justice and peace. Both types of knowledge have great worth and can help us understand more about ourselves as Jews.

The Israelite Tribes and Their Neighbors

DAN Area of Israelite tribes
HIVITES Non-Israelite people

PHOENICIANS
HIVITES
ARAMEANS
Hazor
CANAANITES
ASHER
NAPHTALI
ZEBULUN
Sea of Galilee
ISSACHAR
Mediterranean Sea
CANAANITES MANASSEH
Beth-Shean
Shechem
Jordan River
EPHRAIM
Jaffa
Shiloh
GAD
AMMONITES
DAN BENJAMIN
Ashkelon
Jerusalem
CANAANITES
REUBEN
Gaza PHILISTINES
Hebron
Dead Sea
JUDAH
MOABITES
SIMEON
EDOMITES
AMALEKITES

N
W E
S

0   30 MI
0   50 KM

The early Israelites were divided into twelve tribes, each with its own portion of land.

barley, of grape vines and figs and pomegran-ates, a land of olive trees and honey, a land where you can eat food without limit" (Deuteronomy 8:8).

Each autumn, farmers plowed and sowed before the rains. Their hard work was rewarded in the spring, first with the barley harvest and a few weeks afterward with the wheat harvest. In late summer, farmers gathered the grape harvest. By late September and early October, the olive harvest reached its peak. Men were in charge of the crops and animals. In addition to helping with this work, women spun wool and wove clothes.

The Gift of Monotheism

The religions of the Israelites' neighbors were based on polytheism, or the worship of numer-ous gods. Many of the Canaanite gods were associated with different forces in nature. Yam was the sea god; Shapash, the sun goddess; and Yareach, the moon god. The Canaanites believed that their gods competed against one another for power and for the loyalty of human beings.

The Israelites rejected the idea of many gods with humanlike needs and desires. Instead, they based their religion on monotheism, the idea that there is one God. The Torah helps us understand the values and beliefs of the Israelites. Its teachings go beyond legal concerns for property and the protection of consumers. The Torah commanded the Israelites to treat others with fairness and justice—to care for the widow and the orphan, act kindly toward strangers, and provide food and shelter for the poor. These shared values and beliefs helped distinguish the Israelites from their neighbors. They also helped unite the Israelites.

This statue of the Canaanite god Ba'al is from 1300 BCE. Many Israelites worshipped both Ba'al and the one Jewish God.

Monotheism took hold gradually, for few people change their beliefs and habits overnight. Remember that our ancestors lived in a world filled with religions based on poly-theism. So, at first, many Israelites worshipped Canaanite gods alongside the one Israelite God. Only after centuries of diversity and experi-mentation did they fully accept monotheism.

What Do You Think?

Many say that monotheism is the Jews' greatest gift to civilization. Why might the belief in one God who cares about the well-being of people be considered so valuable?

A Conflict of Cultures

Imagine that you are an Israelite farmer. You live in a land where rain is the key to your survival and where many of your neighbors worship Ba'al, the god of fertility and storms. Why might you feel pressured to also worship Ba'al despite your belief in one God?

Because I stick to my beliefs. I don't care what other people are doing.

How does the experience of an Israelite farmer compare with your experience of living in a multicultural society? For example, describe a conflict you have experienced between your secular and religious values and how you handled the conflict.

I would encounter that I can't have anyone come over on Monday or Wednesday.

Today, Jews around the world express their faith in one God by affixing a mezuzah on the doorposts of their synagogues, homes, and even places of business. Inside every mezuzah is a scroll that includes the words of the Sh'ma: "Hear O Israel, Adonai is our God, Adonai is One."

Chapter 1

The Early Israelites
Adapting to a Changing World

investigate

- How did our ancestors adapt to their new surroundings?
- What made it possible for them to maintain their religious identities?
- How have their lives influenced ours?

Key Words and Places

Judges	Babylonian Kingdom
Philistines	Exile
Jerusalem	Prophets
Holy Temple	Diaspora
Israel	Persians
Judah	Second Temple
Assyria	

The BIG Picture

Every year, when you enter a new grade, your life changes. You have new teachers, classmates, subjects, and lunch choices, maybe even a new school. To adjust, you may need to change. You may need to become more disciplined in studying, or be less picky about what you eat, or wake up earlier to get to school on time.

Just like individuals, communities often face the need to change. In fact, Jewish history is filled with such situations. It began with our ancestors. At first, local chieftains led the Israelites. When they could no longer provide adequate leadership, the Israelites united under a king. Over time, the Israelite kingdom was built, split in two, and destroyed. Many Israelites were forced out of our homeland. Some returned to rebuild it, while others continued to live in foreign lands.

But despite the numerous adaptations, our ancestors maintained their core religious beliefs and identities. While other ancient peoples were conquered, absorbed into the larger culture, and disappeared, the Israelites continued to survive and thrive. How the Jewish people continue to adapt and flourish is what this book is all about.

1200–1050 BCE	about 950 BCE	928 BCE	776 BCE
Settlement of Canaan by Israelites, according to Bible	First Temple built	Kingdom of Israel divided into two ministates: Israel and Judah	World History: First Olympic Games held in Greece

Time to Unite?

Early Israelite society was tribal. A village could be made up of a single clan, and a group of clans formed a tribe. Local **judges,** or chieftains, ruled over the tribes. Often, one judge had authority over a single tribe. Judges were responsible for settling disputes between people and also led their tribes in times of war.

But the neighboring **Philistines** developed superior military technology, such as iron-spoke chariots, and began pushing into Israelite territory. The Israelites needed a more centralized leadership than the local judges could provide. They needed one leader who could unite them in their fight for survival.

And so, the Bible tells us, at God's command, Saul was anointed the first king of Israel. But Saul was more like a tribal chief than a king. The territory he controlled was not very large and he had no palace or capital city. Although he was a great warrior, Saul was unable to unite the Israelites.

722 BCE
- Northern kingdom of Israel destroyed by Assyrians

586 BCE
- Judah defeated by Babylonians; Jerusalem and Temple burned to the ground

539 BCE
- Babylonian Empire falls to Persians

about 516 BCE
- Second Temple dedicated in Jerusalem

445 BCE
- Nehemiah travels to Jerusalem; helps Jews rebuild Judah

Deborah of Lappidoth

The Book of Judges tells of a judge named Deborah: "Deborah, a prophet and the wife of Lappidoth, led Israel at that time. She would sit under the Palm of Deborah...in the hill country of Ephraim, and the Israelites would come up to her for judgments" (Judges 4:4–5).

When the Israelites were attacked by a Canaanite king, they turned to Deborah. She chose a man named Barak to lead the Israelite army, but he didn't want to go without her help. Together, they led the Israelites to victory.

How might Deborah's judgments have been influenced by the Israelite belief in God's concern for people?

Upon her victory in battle, Deborah the prophet sang, "Hear O kings...I will sing to Adonai...the God of Israel" (Judges 5:3).

A Kingdom Is Built but Cracks

It was Israel's second king, David, who succeeded in uniting the Israelites. David fought back the Philistines and also captured the city of **Jerusalem,** establishing it as the kingdom's political and religious capital. During the more than thirty years of his reign, King David unified a bitterly divided people and developed Israel into one of the strongest powers in the region. He fought back the Philistines so that they never again posed a threat to Israel's survival.

The kingdom grew even stronger under the reign of David's son, King Solomon. Solomon centralized Israel's government in Jerusalem and increased its wealth and status by developing Israel into a center of international trade. According to the Bible's book Kings, Solomon fortified many cities and built a wall around Jerusalem. However, he is probably best remembered for his huge construction projects. The most famous was in Jerusalem: the **Holy Temple,** or Beit Hamikdash, which was completed around 950 BCE.

Despite his many accomplishments, King Solomon's reign created religious conflicts and economic problems that weakened the kingdom. When he died, the united kingdom of Israel cracked into two ministates: **Israel** in the north and **Judah** in the south. Without a central government and a strong military, each struggled to survive in a dangerous region. Their struggle increased as a new power arose: the kingdom of **Assyria,** which was in the northeast (modern-day Iraq).

The Book of Samuel tells the story of how, as a young man, David slew the great Philistine warrior Goliath of Gath using only his shepherd's slingshot. The Philistines panicked at the sight of their fallen warrior and they retreated.

Israel and Judah banded together with other small states in the region to prevent the Assyrians from taking control. Unfortunately, they could not withstand the might of the Assyrian army. In 722 BCE, the northern kingdom of Israel was destroyed. According to the Book of Kings, more than twenty-seven thousand Israelites were deported to the interior of the Assyrian Empire. The southern kingdom of Judah was spared when its king agreed to pay the conquering Assyrians a ransom in silver and gold.

Destruction of Judah

The Assyrian kingdom was eventually brought down by rebellious states outside of Judah in the east. But Judah was still sandwiched between two competing powers: Egypt in the south and the **Babylonian kingdom** in the northeast. In 597 BCE, the Babylonian king, Nebuchadnezzar, swept into Judah. He forced King Jehoiakim and the kingdom's spiritual

This stone sculpture shows an Assyrian military officer bringing two Judeans from the town of Lachish to the Assyrian king.

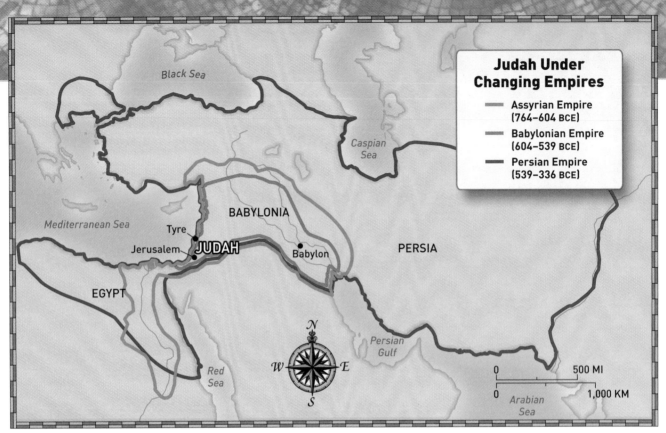

When the northern kingdom of Israel fell to Assyria in 722 BCE and, later on, when the southern kingdom of Judah was conquered by the Babylonians in 586 BCE, many Israelites were exiled to what is now modern-day Iraq and Iran.

leaders and leading citizens out of Judah into **exile**. In addition, he levied heavy taxes on the remaining population. When Judah rebelled a few years later, the Babylonian army returned and laid siege to Jerusalem. In the summer of 586 BCE, Jerusalem and the Temple were burned to the ground.

The Babylonian king Nebuchadnezzar had not just devastated a city and destroyed the Holy Temple—he also destroyed a way of life. For the people of Judah, family, work, and religion had all revolved around the land. Their families had tilled the soil and then paid tribute to God by bringing the fruits of their labor to the Temple in Jerusalem. Now deprived of their Temple, land, and leaders, they had no place to worship

God, no place to farm, and no one to lead them. The impoverished people of Judah and the devastated exiles were like homeless orphans.

A Message of Hope

Before the exile, the **prophets,** such as Amos and Isaiah, had criticized the people for their faithlessness and immoral ways. Now the prophets comforted the Israelites with a message of hope. The God of Israel had not been defeated by the Babylonian gods, Jeremiah taught. Instead God had used Nebuchadnezzar as a tool to punish the Israelites for their sinful ways. The prophet Ezekiel held out hope that

The Prophet Elijah

In the difficult years between Solomon's death and the Temple's destruction, "prophets" arose among the Israelites. The prophets saw themselves as called upon by God to speak God's word. They taught God's ethical teachings—such as the values of justice, honesty, and tzedakah. Sometimes, they also predicted the future and gave kings political advice.

What would you do if a president or other politician in your country were abusing power and behaving unethically? If you were a prophet, you would speak up. That made the job of prophet dangerous. The prophet Elijah experienced this danger firsthand.

King Ahab of Israel and his wife, Queen Jezebel, enriched themselves at the expense of their subjects. They also encouraged Israelites to worship idols and the Canaanite god Ba'al alongside God. Elijah spoke up, criticizing Ahab and Jezebel. By doing so he took an enormous risk. Unlike previous kings who had respected the prophets and treated them as trusted advisers, Ahab called Elijah "my enemy" and a "troubler of Israel." Elijah was forced to flee the northern kingdom of Israel.

How can Elijah's courage be a model for you? For example, if you saw a bully taking advantage of another student, what would you do?

_____

_____

_____

By the Rivers of Babylon

"By the rivers of Babylon, there we sat and wept, as we remembered Zion [Jerusalem]."

These famous words from Psalm 137 express the exiles' heartbreak. How could God have allowed the Holy Land and Temple—God's dwelling place—to be destroyed? Many still believed that specific gods had power over specific places. So, they questioned if it was possible to worship the God of Israel outside of Israel. Could the God of Israel hear them from far away, from the banks of the Tigris and the Euphrates?

Far from all that was familiar to them and living among strangers, the Israelites were often unhappy, even fearful. Have you ever been far from home, for example at camp, or ever moved to a new neighborhood or attended a new school? What did it feel like the first few days or months? Why?

_____

_____

_____

What helped you adapt to your new surroundings?

_____

_____

_____

_____

Today, the prophets continue to comfort us. This sign in Israel's Ben-Gurion Airport includes Jeremiah's words of hope, "Your children shall return to their country" (Jeremiah 31:17). It reminds us that the Jewish people wait for the return of Israeli MIAs— soldiers who are missing in action.

the exiles would return to Israel, saying: "Thus said Adonai God:... O my people, [I shall] bring you [back] to the Land of Israel…. I shall put My breath in you, and you will live again" (Ezekiel 37:13–14).

There was another great prophet of the exile, whose name has been lost to history. His prophesies make up the final chapters of the Book of Isaiah. This prophet assured the people that God would hear their prayers in exile. God, he also taught, was the God of all people, regardless of their religion or where they lived: "Your redeemer is the Holy One of Israel, who is called 'God of all the Earth'" (Isaiah 54:5).

Today, we take it for granted that people can worship God from anywhere. But in the time of exile, it was a new idea. It was an idea that would help the Jewish people survive and even prosper in a new land.

Life in Exile

For over twenty-five hundred years, many Jews have lived in the **Diaspora,** or countries outside of Israel. In fact, living in the Diaspora feels normal to Jews today. But for the Jews in Babylonia, it was a huge adjustment, much as it would be a staggering change for us if most of the people living in the United States or Canada were sent to live in Latin America.

The prophets recognized the importance of helping the exiles return to the normal routines of life. Jeremiah sent a letter from Jerusalem to the Jews in Babylon. In God's name, he urged them: "Build houses and live in them. Plant gardens and eat their fruits. Take wives and bear sons and daughters…. Multiply there, do not decrease in numbers. And seek peace for the city to which I [God] have exiled you, and pray to Adonai in its behalf; for in its peace you will have peace" (Jeremiah 29:5–7).

The exiles took Jeremiah's words to heart. They set up communities within the larger non-Jewish population, taking part in business and even politics.

To Stay or Not to Stay?

In 539 BCE, the Babylonian Empire fell to the **Persians**. Fortunately for the Jews, the Persian ruler, King Cyrus, went out of his way to show respect to his new subjects' gods. To gain support and favor with the Jews, Cyrus permitted the exiles to return to Judah and rebuild the Temple.

Despite their joy in hearing this news, most Jews chose not to resettle in Judah. The journey would be dangerous, and life in Judah was difficult now that it had become an isolated province of a large empire. In contrast, Babylon was a thriving capital city.

Who might have used this ancient pitcher and necklace? Perhaps someone your age poured water from the pitcher. Perhaps someone who returned to Judah from Babylonia wore the necklace.

Returning and Rebuilding

The first Jews to return to Judah began rebuilding the Beit Hamikdash. The **Second Temple** was completed in about 516 BCE, seventy years after the destruction of the First Temple (the Temple that Solomon built). The dedication was celebrated with great joy. It was also touched with sadness for those old enough to remember the splendor of the original Temple. The modest building that now stood in its place paled in comparison.

The next fifty years were difficult for the people of Judah. The Persians were willing to let Jews live in the land, but they would never permit an independent Jewish government. Judah remained poor and sparsely populated.

In 458 BCE, Judah was invigorated when a scribe and religious leader named Ezra led nearly fifteen hundred Jews back from Babylonia. Ezra was determined to revitalize the religious life of Judah. Empowered by the

Persian government, he appointed judges and officials to teach the laws of the Torah and to make rulings based on them.

Ezra sent word to the Jewish community in Babylonia about the difficult conditions in Judah. Nehemiah, who was the highest-ranking Jewish official in the Persian court, was disturbed by what he heard. He convinced the Persian king to make him governor of Judah. Shortly after Nehemiah arrived in Jerusalem, he set the entire city to work as an emergency force to rebuild Jerusalem's destroyed walls. No longer would the city be raided or threatened by neighboring enemies.

Nehemiah also rebuilt Judah's economy. He ordered a onetime cancellation of all debts and restored the annual Temple taxes. Nehemiah understood that economic revival would require making Jerusalem into an urban center.

The city's population was too small to support the changes Nehemiah wanted to make. So he resettled 10 percent of Judah's rural population in the city.

New Challenges Ahead

Judah made a strong comeback under the leadership of Ezra and Nehemiah. The population of Jerusalem increased and was revitalized. Not only had the Jews figured out how to survive in the Diaspora but they also demonstrated an unbreakable tie to the Land of Israel.

But then as now, empires rise and fall, and Jewish communities often are deeply affected by these shifts in power. The rise of an extraordinary leader in the Diaspora was about to bring Jews under the control of the Greek Empire. New challenges were on the horizon.

A Tradition of Innovation

Reading Torah aloud in synagogue is a time-honored tradition today. But at one time it was an innovation. It began with a public Torah reading by Ezra in 444 BCE.

Imagine the scene: Massive groups of people come to Jerusalem and gather around a wooden platform. Slowly, Ezra makes his way up the platform. As he opens the scroll, men, women, and children rise as one. The crowd hangs on every word Ezra reads from the Torah—these are the beliefs that unite the Jewish people. "Amen, amen," the people cry.

Because the Judeans spoke Aramaic, they needed translators to help them understand the Hebrew text of the Torah. Similarly, we now use English translations of the Torah. Describe another way that your synagogue helps its members participate in Jewish life.

_____

_____

Why do you think we continue to read from the Torah as part of our synagogue prayer services? Who reads from the Torah in your synagogue—the rabbi, cantor, or congregants?

then & NOW

The Babylonians did not discriminate against the Jews because of their religion or nationality. This helped the Jews achieve economic success. It also encouraged them to adopt the culture of their new land.

Some Jews not only adapted to their surroundings, but also abandoned Judaism. Still, many remained faithful. Religious rituals such as observing Shabbat, keeping kosher, and performing a circumcision, or *brit milah,* took on new importance. In addition, Jewish communities came together by gathering for communal prayer at city gates or near lakes and rivers. These practices eventually gained widespread acceptance. They further unified the Jews and strengthened their religious and cultural identities.

1. What secular holidays or traditions help you identify with all the citizens of your country?

_____

_____

2. What religious holidays or traditions help you identify with other Jews?

_____

_____

3. Imagine a Jewish community living one hundred years from now. Describe one belief or tradition you think they are likely to have in common with you. Why do you think so?

_____

_____

Chapter 2

The Age of Hellenism

Diverse Strategies for Survival

investigate

- What were the temptations for Jews to adopt the ways of their new rulers even when they conflicted with Jewish values and culture?

- What helped Jews resist the temptation and maintain their Jewish identities?

- How do our lives in today's Diaspora mirror those of our ancestors?

Key Words and Places

Judea	Septuagint
Hellenism	Seleucid Kingdom
Ptolemies	Maccabees
Archaeologists	

The **BIG** Picture

In 331 BCE, less than two hundred years after the rebuilding of the Temple, Jerusalem was conquered by Alexander the Great. Alexander was King of Macedonia and one of the greatest military geniuses who has ever lived. By the time he died, Alexander's empire stretched from Greece to India. A lover of Greek culture, Alexander aimed to unite his empire by blending Greek culture with local customs, religions, and traditions.

Like other peoples who were conquered by Alexander, the Jews felt conflicted. On the one hand, Hellenistic culture was exciting and advanced. On the other, it threatened the traditional ways of life the Jews valued.

331 BCE	323 BCE	200 BCE	about 169 BCE
Alexander the Great conquers Jerusalem	Alexander dies; Egypt and Judea placed under control of Ptolemy	Judea becomes part of the Seleucid Empire	Jews rebel against Menelaus, the High Priest, and Antiochus Epiphanes, the Seleucid King

Changing Times

Imagine you were living in the Land of Israel around 225 BCE, about a century after Alexander the Great died. What kinds of changes might you see in your everyday life? The first would be that Judah would now be known by its Greek and Roman name, **Judea.** Other signs of **Hellenism,** or the blending of Greek culture with the local culture, may have appeared in the form of decorated Greek vases sold on market day in the larger villages. Or perhaps Jewish soldiers who served in the army would bring back gifts of Greek clothing, perfumes, and jewelry.

Greek culture did not conquer the Ancient Near East as quickly as Alexander's army had. Hellenism spread gradually and unevenly.

It was strongest in urban areas where the population came in contact with Greek soldiers and merchants, and where Greek was adopted as the language in which to conduct business. It is natural that the more frequently people come in contact with an idea, language, or culture, the more quickly they adopt it.

164 BCE

Maccabees capture Jerusalem from Seleucids; Temple purified and rededicated

141 BCE

Seleucids defeated by Hasmoneans; Judea independent again

about 100 BCE

World History:
Anasazi Native American culture first develops in what is now Arizona and New Mexico

By introducing Greek culture to the Middle East, Alexander the Great had a tremendous influence on the development of Judaism.

Remaining Connected

After Alexander died, in 323 BCE, his empire was divided among three of his generals—Ptolemy, Lysimachus, and Seleucus. Egypt and Judea were placed under the control of Ptolemy. He and his successors, known as the **Ptolemies,** were tolerant rulers. The Ptolemies wanted to modernize the agriculturally rich Nile valley. Seeking prosperity, great numbers of Jews flocked to Egypt. Like other immigrants, they were protected and favored because they worked in the king's service. There were Jewish agricultural laborers, metalworkers, weavers, and merchants. Many Jews were also soldiers in the Ptolemaic army.

The Jews living in Egypt and other Diaspora communities along the Mediterranean were, in

Just as Jewish women wove cloth for centuries in the Land of Israel, so, too, did many of them weave cloth in Hellenistic Alexandria.

Greek colonists brought their literature, theater, sporting competitions, and religious festivals to many of the conquered cities. Greek temples, amphitheaters, and schools began to dot the city landscapes. The cultural offerings in newly established "Greek" cities, such as Alexandria in Egypt, attracted Jews and non-Jews alike.

Hellenism came far more slowly to rural areas of Judea, where farmers had less contact with the Greek colonists and their institutions. Even so, all Jews in Judea felt the impact of Hellenism's reach.

An archaeologist is a person who studies the artifacts, or remnants, of earlier cultures. The artifacts, which often have become buried over time, may include items such as tools, wall paintings, and pottery. Archaeologists help us learn about history and the lives of the people who came before us.

a number of ways, like North American Jews today. They lived near one another so that they could participate in religious and Jewish communal life. They also gathered together in "prayer houses." Although **archaeologists** and historians don't know exactly what went on in the prayer houses, some think prayer houses were the forerunners of synagogues.

Like most Jews of today's Diaspora, Hellenist Jews also adapted to their surroundings. This included adopting the Greek language and style

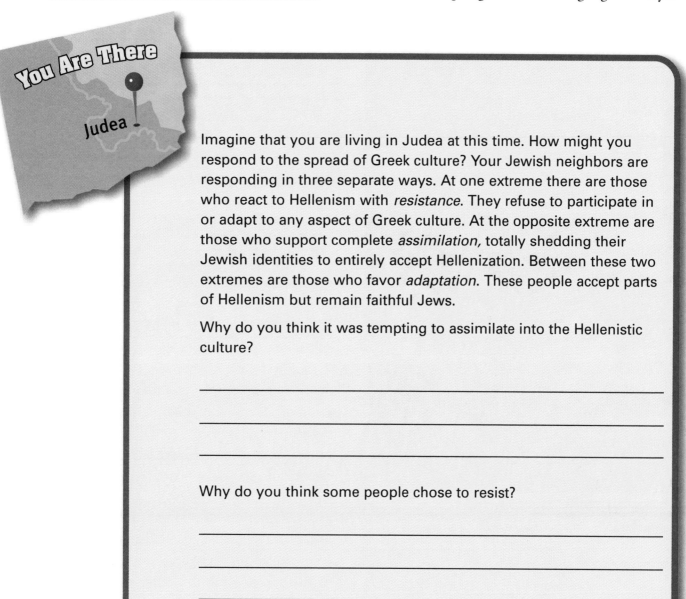

You Are There

Judea

Imagine that you are living in Judea at this time. How might you respond to the spread of Greek culture? Your Jewish neighbors are responding in three separate ways. At one extreme there are those who react to Hellenism with *resistance*. They refuse to participate in or adapt to any aspect of Greek culture. At the opposite extreme are those who support complete *assimilation,* totally shedding their Jewish identities to entirely accept Hellenization. Between these two extremes are those who favor *adaptation*. These people accept parts of Hellenism but remain faithful Jews.

Why do you think it was tempting to assimilate into the Hellenistic culture?

_____

_____

_____

Why do you think some people chose to resist?

_____

_____

_____

The Greek Torah: Septuagint

Hellenism had a strong impact on the Jewish communities of the Diaspora; it even influenced the way they practiced Judaism. As a result of adopting Greek as their language, for example, many Jews grew up without learning to speak and read Hebrew. So, just as translators interpreted and explained the Hebrew text of the Torah in Aramaic in the time of Ezra, the Jews now adapted by translating the Torah into Greek. The written translation is called the Septuagint. By translating their most sacred book, the Jews could keep Jewish traditions and values alive and pass their religion on to the next generation.

The Septuagint made it possible for Jews who did not know Hebrew to read and understand the Torah. But not everyone supported the idea of translating the Torah. Many Jews argued that the Torah could not be translated without losing much of its meaning, because each Hebrew word had been chosen by God.

At prayer services in your synagogue, would you miss the English translation of the prayers and Torah reading if they were not included? Why or why not?

of dress, and giving their children Greek names and sending them to Greek-style schools.

Despite their adaptation to Greek culture, many Diaspora Jews maintained their ties to Judaism and to the Jews of Judea. Their relationship can be compared to that of today's North American Jews with Israeli Jews. On the one hand, we have many shared values and traditions, such as the value of studying Torah and celebrating the High Holidays. On the other hand, we have many distinct traditions. In contrast to the Diaspora, in the modern State of Israel the Torah is taught in secular schools and religious schools, and Jewish life is strongly controlled by the government.

Conflict in Judea

The **Seleucid kingdom,** named for Alexander's former general Seleucus, was based in Syria. It was formed out of the eastern portion of Alexander's empire. Judea lay on the edge of the Ptolemaic and Seleucid kingdoms. The two kingdoms continually battled over where the boundary line between them should be drawn. In 200 BCE, the Seleucids gained control over Judea.

At first, daily life in Judea continued as before. But trouble was brewing. A conflict broke out between the High Priest Onias (Ḥanan) and his younger brother Jason (Joshua). Onias wanted to limit the influence of Hellenism in Jerusalem, while Jason wanted to turn Jerusalem into a Greek-style city to bring it wealth and culture.

Then, in 175 BCE a new ruler, Antiochus Epiphanes, rose to the Seleucid throne. He quickly earned the hatred of the Judeans by doubling their taxes. Realizing that Antiochus was starved for cash, Jason bribed the king to make him High Priest instead of his brother. Jason's move caused a stir in Judea, for the position of High Priest traditionally was passed down from father to eldest son. With Antiochus's blessing, Jason further divided the population by making Jerusalem into a Greek-style city, building a sports arena next to the Temple. Some of the younger priests neglected their duties because they preferred to take part in the neighboring athletic competitions. Traditional Jews were horrified and vowed to resist Hellenism.

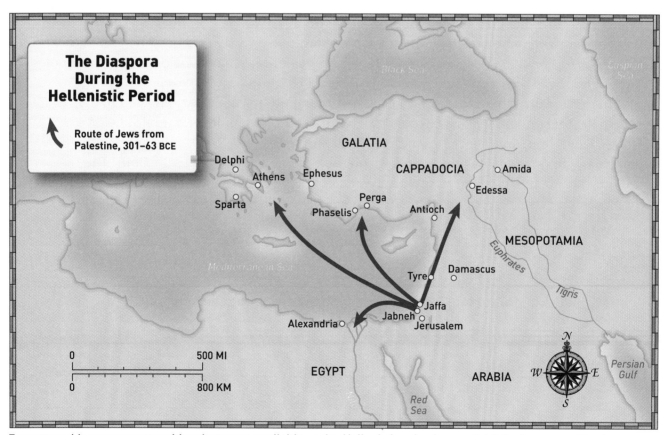

Encouraged by new opportunities that were available under Hellenistic rule, Jews established communities in modern-day Egypt, Greece, and Turkey.

These glass bottles are from the time of the Second Temple. Like other ancient artifacts, they were made by hand, not machine. How do they compare with the glass bottles and vases in your home?

The Revolt Against Antiochus

Despite Jason's attraction to Greek culture, his Hellenism program had limits. He continued to respect the holiness of the Temple and did not interfere with sacrifices and other rituals. But soon after Jason's appointment, a more extreme Hellenist named Menelaus offered Antiochus an even larger bribe than Jason had given. The result: Jason was out as High Priest and Menelaus was in.

Whereas Jason favored adaptation, Menelaus believed in assimilation. Thus, tensions were

Lawless or Enlightened?

When people's points of view are at opposite extremes, what is described as lawless by one person may be seen as enlightened, or forward thinking, by another. The text below is from the First Book of Maccabees 1:11–15. (The Book of Maccabees belongs to a group of ancient texts that were not included in the Bible.)

"In those days there arose in Israel lawless men [led by Jason] who misled many, saying, 'Let us go and make a covenant with the heathen [people who do not believe in God—Hellenizers] around us....' And they built a gymnasium [Greek-style sports arena] in Jerusalem, in heathen fashion..., and abandoned the holy covenant [with God]. They united with the heathen and became servants of evil."

Based on this passage, describe the writer's view of Hellenism.

_____

_____

Rewrite the quote as a Hellenist Jew might have described the situation.

_____

_____

_____

_____

 **Sound Familiar?**

Corruption in High Places

Are you surprised that Temple priests became corrupt? Today, as in biblical times, people in positions of authority sometimes misuse their power.

Name three qualities that you look for in a leader as proof of the person's trustworthiness.

1. _____

2. _____

3. _____

Write a classified ad for Menelaus's replacement as High Priest. Describe the character of the person you want to hire and what that person's approach to Hellenism must be.

_____

_____

_____

If you had to write a classified ad for a rabbi to work in a summer camp, how would your description of the rabbi be the same as the High Priest's? How would it be different?

Same	**Different**
_____	_____
_____	_____
_____	_____
_____	_____

already high when Menelaus stole holy vessels from the Temple and arranged to have Onias killed. In 169 BCE, Menelaus's opponents, led by Jason, revolted. Judea descended into civil war.

Antiochus considered the uprising to be a revolt against his rule. He marched into Jerusalem with troops, slaughtered many of the protesters, and sold others into slavery. Antiochus looted the Temple and entered the Holy of Holies—a place forbidden to all but the High Priest on Yom Kippur. Jerusalem became an occupied city, with a new military fortress overlooking the Temple.

"The Hammer"

Antiochus was still not satisfied. Considering the Jews to be a disruptive force in his empire, he forbade the observance of Jewish rituals, Shabbat, and holidays. He outlawed the study of Torah and converted the Beit Hamikdash into a Greek temple. He placed a statue of Zeus near the altar and even ordered the sacrifice of pigs in the Temple.

For the next two years, a country priest named Mattathias the Hasmonean, along with members of his resistance, fought a guerrilla war against the Seleucids. Although they were outnumbered and had only primitive weapons, the rebels had the advantage of knowing the land of Judea. They knew the best routes to take and where to hide. Another advantage they had was the secret aid of a sympathetic Jewish population.

After Mattathias died, his son Judah took command of the rebels. Judah's men nicknamed their bold leader "Maccabee," which means "hammer." The rebels became known as **Maccabees**. They lived up to their name, dealing hammer blow after hammer blow to the Seleucids. But Judah's victories were modest, in comparison to those that could be achieved by a large and sophisticated army.

Ḥanukkah

In the Jewish month of Kislev in 164 BCE, the Maccabees captured Jerusalem from the Seleucids and purified the Temple. The Temple was rededicated on the twenty-fifth day of Kislev, the third anniversary of the day it had been defiled by Antiochus.

Judah and his men styled their dedication after the eight-day festival of Sukkot, which they had not been able to celebrate a few months earlier. The new festival eventually became known as Ḥanukkah, which means "dedication." To this day, Ḥanukkah begins on the twenty-fifth day of Kislev, which usually falls in December, and is celebrated for eight days.

On Hanukkah, we eat foods cooked in oil, such as potato latkes and sufganiyot—jelly doughnuts. This custom honors the tradition that the oil in the rededicated Temple's candlestick miraculously lasted for eight days.

Independence and Division

The Hasmoneans' struggle to win independence from the Seleucids continued for another twenty-three years. In 141 BCE, the hated Seleucid fortress overlooking the Temple was finally destroyed. The Jews were free once again.

Judah Maccabee

Judah Maccabee was a great military leader who conducted an early form of guerrilla warfare. Because the Seleucid forces were superior in both numbers and arms, Judah avoided open battle. He and his band of rebels executed a series of daring and successful night attacks that made use of their superior knowledge of the land.

Judah died on the battlefield in 161 BCE. His brothers succeeded him, securing the independence of Judea twenty years later.

Use the space below to draw a picture or write a poem that portrays the courage of Judah and his band of followers.

Judah Maccabee and his followers armed themselves with captured weapons.

The Origin of the Oil Story

A legend recorded in the Talmud suggests another reason why the Hasmoneans, the family that led the revolt against the Greeks, created an eight-day festival. When the Maccabees purified the Beit Hamikdash, this story says, they found enough oil to light the Temple's branched candlestick for only one day. According to the story, the oil miraculously lasted for eight days.

Hebrew and Greek and some included symbols that were not uniquely Jewish, such as anchors, palm trees, and wheels.

North American Jews continue to face the issue of resisting, assimilating, or adapting to Diaspora cultures. But it hasn't divided us to the same extent that it divided the Jews of Judea. Under the Hasmoneans the bitter divisions would bring tragic consequences.

Mattathias's only surviving son, Simon, was proclaimed High Priest and Prince of the People. This signaled a change from the past because Simon was not a member of the traditional high priestly family. In the minds of some Jews, he was no more a legitimate High Priest than Menelaus had been. Simon's grandson would go one step farther and proclaim himself king of the Jews, a position that many Jews believed could only be held by a descendant of King David.

Although Judea was independent, it was still part of a region dominated by Hellenism. So the question Jews continued to face was: Do you support resistance, assimilation, or adaptation? Ironically, the descendants of the Maccabees were in favor of adaptation. For example, they minted coins that used both

This Hasmonean coin has a Jewish symbol. It is a seven-branched menorah, a symbol of the Temple's branched candlestick. If you were creating a coin for the modern State of Israel, what symbol would you put on it? Why?

A conflict of values caused disunity among the Jews under Hellenistic rule. Those who were drawn to Hellenism and wanted to assimilate pointed to the greatness of Greek philosophy, literature, and theater. They valued the excitement of Greek athletic competitions and the richness and beauty of Greek culture. Those who resisted Hellenism argued that the Greeks had an inferior culture. They argued that the Greeks glorified war, oppressed the poor, and indulged in drunkenness and idolatry. They saw Hellenism as a direct threat to Judaism.

In modern times, the conflicts of assimilation versus resistance or adaptation are also most intense during the month of December, when both Ḥanukkah and Christmas are celebrated.

1. Why do you think this issue continues to be a problem for Jews?

_____

_____

_____

_____

2. What suggestion(s) do you have for addressing the problem?

_____

_____

_____

_____

Chapter **3**

Roman Domination of Judea

Divisions Inside and Out

investigate

- Why did the differences among our ancestors cause conflict?

- How did their intolerance bring them to the verge of destruction?

- What can we learn from them so that we use our differences to strengthen the Jewish community?

Key Words and Places

Essenes	Messiah
Sadducees	Sicarii
Pharisees	Zealots
Crucifixion	Tisha B'Av
Masada	Sinat Ḥinam
Procurators	

The **BIG** Picture

Judea was flourishing. Thanks to Hasmonean conquests, the Jewish state grew to include almost all of biblical Israel as well as land east of the Jordan River and the southern Golan. The Hasmoneans controlled profitable trade routes, and merchants and large landowners thrived. But the less prosperous Judeans carried the heavy tax burden required to maintain Judea's large army. In addition, resentment of the Hasmoneans grew when they forced the non-Jews in their kingdom to convert to Judaism.

While this was a time of great Jewish diversity—political, economic, and religious—it was also a time of intolerance for difference. One group went so far as to distance itself from other Jews by moving to the desert. Another used guerrilla tactics to intimidate those who opposed them. These deep divisions would have been disastrous in the best of times. But these were hardly the best of times. In fact, the Jews were about to battle the most powerful empire the world had ever seen.

---

63 BCE
Roman general Pompey makes Judea a Roman province

37 BCE
Romans name Herod "king of the Jews"

10 BCE
Hillel and Shammai teach in Jerusalem

6 CE
Zadok and Judah the Galilean lead tax revolt against Romans

Judea Divided

The Hasmoneans wanted to recapture the glory days of King David and King Solomon. But their devotion to conquering territory and their desire to rule the Jewish State like the neighboring Hellenistic kingdoms only heightened divisions within the population. Conflict increased between the rich and the poor, Jews and non-Jews, passionate Hellenizers and traditionalists.

The situation reached a low point in around 90 BCE. The Hasmonean king Alexander Yannai was performing a Sukkot ceremony in the Temple. Suddenly, the people began to pelt him with *etrogim*, or citrons. Why would the Jews attack their king?

One reason lay in the Hasmonean kings' decision to declare themselves both High Priests and kings. Until then, there had been a separation of religious and political leadership. Many also resented the high taxes the king required to support his numerous military campaigns.

The first to voice their opposition to the concentration of power in the hands of the Hasmoneans were the **Essenes**. They led simple lives that emphasized religious ideals and the study of Torah in minute detail. Wanting nothing to do with the Hasmonean leader, or "Wicked Priest," as they called him, they moved to the Judean desert, founding the settlement of Qumran by the edge of the Dead Sea.

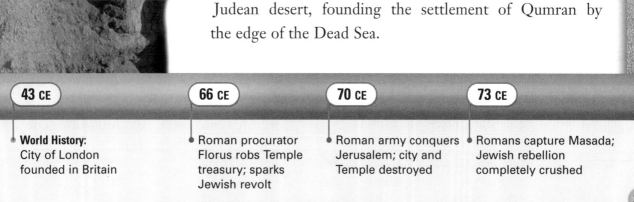

43 CE	**66 CE**	**70 CE**	**73 CE**
World History: City of London founded in Britain	Roman procurator Florus robs Temple treasury; sparks Jewish revolt	Roman army conquers Jerusalem; city and Temple destroyed	Romans capture Masada; Jewish rebellion completely crushed

Rather than head for the desert, other groups stayed in Judea and struggled for power. Two major rivals—actually religious and political parties—developed. They were the **Sadducees** and the **Pharisees**. The two differed largely in their social and economic makeup and in their approach to understanding Torah.

The Sadducees were mostly wealthy priests and aristocrats. They traditionally filled the religious and political leadership roles in Jerusalem. The Pharisees included both priests and nonpriests, rich and poor Jews alike. Most Jews, however, were not members of either party. Most Jews were poor farmers, craftspeople, and fishermen who did not have the leisure to think about the political schemes of rival groups.

The Pharisees wanted to replace the current leadership because they believed that the powers of the king and priest should be separated. Understandably, kings do not look favorably on people who talk about replacing them. So, the Hasmonean rulers sided with the Sadducees. That caused the Pharisees to increase their opposition. From there, things quickly turned ugly.

The End of Independence

This brings us back to the unfortunate *etrogim* incident in the Temple—it was the Pharisees who led the revolt against King Alexander Yannai. Yannai struck back using a slow and painful Roman execution technique called **crucifixion** in which the condemned are hung on a cross. He tortured many of his political opponents through crucifixion.

After Yannai's death, the Pharisees regained political influence. Soon after, they attacked the Sadducees. Unfortunately, the Jews were so busy fighting a civil war that they ignored a much more serious threat: the expanding Roman Empire. In 63 BCE, the Roman general Pompey marched into Jerusalem and ended the civil war by making Judea a Roman province.

Herod the Great?

Now Judea was under the authority of Rome. At first, Roman rule was not very different from the rule of the Hasmoneans. Roman leaders were mainly concerned with collecting taxes and keeping the peace. They were content to let a Jewish leader rule the Land of Israel, as long as he remained loyal to Rome. In 37 BCE, the Romans named Herod "king of the Jews." Herod was a general whose family had been forcibly converted to Judaism generations earlier by the Hasmoneans.

Pharisees and Sadducees

In first-century Judea, there was no clear separation between politics and religion the way there is in the United States and Canada today. The Pharisees and the Sadducees were competing political groups. They also had very different religious beliefs.

The Pharisees believed that the written Torah could only be understood in combination with an oral tradition—teachings passed on by word of mouth. As scholars who were learned in both the written and the oral traditions, the Pharisees considered themselves the natural leaders of the people.

The Sadducees, many of whom were members of the High Priest's family, rejected the Pharisees' oral tradition. They argued that the priests, whom the Torah specified as the religious leaders, were the only ones qualified to interpret the Torah.

Digging Up the Past

One morning in 1947, a Bedouin shepherd made one of the most important archaeological discoveries of the twentieth century. In a cave near the Dead Sea he found a group of ceramic jars. Inside were leathery scrolls, many of which turned out to be ancient copies of biblical books, such as the Book of Isaiah.

Known as the Dead Sea Scrolls, these are the oldest copies of biblical texts ever discovered. Scholars believe it was the Essenes who put the scrolls in these caves. The Essenes lived next to the caves, in the settlement of Qumran.

Some of the scrolls teach us about the Essenes. Their community was organized as a commune—a collective in which there is no private property and work is shared equally. Life centered on community meals and prayer.

This scroll of the Book of Isaiah was found in Qumran. Just like Torah scrolls, it has no vowels. Do you recognize any of the Hebrew letters or words?

The archaeological remains of King Herod's palace include remnants of a tower, a courtyard with columns, and a synagogue.

A strong leader, Herod brought over thirty years of calm to the Land of Israel. He was a master builder of cities and fortresses. He rebuilt Jerusalem and expanded the Beit Hamikdash into one of the most beautiful and impressive temples in the Roman Empire. Even the Pharisees, who hated Herod, were forced to admit, "Anyone who has not seen Herod's building has never seen a building that is truly grand."

But Herod often seemed not to care about the Jews. His loyalty was to the Romans. In fact, he placed a large Roman eagle—the symbol of Rome's might—on the Temple gate. When two Pharisees tore it down, Herod had them burned alive. He also deepened the divisions among Jews, and his building programs were costly, the heavy tax burden bringing many farmers to the edge of ruin.

Perhaps most destructive were Herod's fits of violence. He went so far as to murder most of

Famous FIGURES

Hillel and Shammai

Two of the most famous Pharisees were Hillel and Shammai, both of whom lived during the time of Herod the Great. Hillel and Shammai were both revered teachers but they often differed in their interpretations of the Torah. The following Talmudic story highlights differences in the temperaments of these two famous teachers.

How can greeting others with a smile rather than a frown be a way to follow Hillel's teaching?

One day, a non-Jew came before Shammai and said, "I will convert to Judaism if you teach me the whole Torah while standing on one foot." Shammai responded by chasing the man away with a stick. The man then went before Hillel and repeated his challenge. Hillel responded, "What is hateful to you, do not do to others. That is the entire Torah. The rest is commentary. Now go and study [Torah]."

Whose response do you think was more appropriate? Why?

_____

_____

Describe one way you can apply Hillel's teaching in your everyday life.

_____

_____

his family, suspecting they were plotting against him. He executed many popular figures—including his wife, the Hasmonean princess Miriamne. Fearing attempts on his throne and life, Herod built massive fortresses where he could escape in case of rebellion. The most famous fortress was **Masada**.

Challenging the Romans

Herod succeeded in stifling opposition because the people feared him. But soon after he died, in 4 BCE, farmers rose up in protest. Many had been forced off their farms because they could not pay their taxes. Now some became Robin Hood-style bandits, stealing weapons, looting royal palaces, robbing travelers, and even attacking Roman soldiers.

The Romans soon took direct control of Judea and clamped down on the bandits. (The Galilee and Golan remained under the control of Herod's sons.) The Roman Senate appointed special commissioners, called **procurators,** to tend to military, judicial, and civil matters. The High Priest controlled religious affairs and other local matters. The Romans auctioned off the office of High Priest to the highest bidder, who was usually a Sadducee. Many poorer people resented the close relationship between the Sadducees and the Romans, so they turned to the Pharisees as their religious and political leaders.

But even the Pharisees were not fully united on the issue of Roman control of Judea. Some were violently opposed to Roman rule. In 6 CE, a Pharisee named Zadok and a popular community leader named Judah the Galilean led a tax revolt against the Romans. Others did not openly oppose the Romans; instead, they prayed to God to send a savior.

Praying for the Messiah

In these troubled times, many Jews turned to God for relief. Some believed that God would send a messiah to destroy their enemies and rule them as in the days of old. So they prayed for the coming of the Messiah, for the "End of Days"—the end of their suffering and the start of a more perfect world.

The Hebrew word for messiah, *mashiah,* means "anointed one." In biblical times, kings were anointed with oil. Thus, many people expected the Messiah to be a flesh-and-blood king.

The Golden Gate is located at the south wall of the Temple District of Jerusalem. According to tradition, the Messiah will enter the city through this gate. In 1541 CE, the arches were sealed by the Muslim ruler, Ottoman Sultan Suleiman I, to prevent the Messiah from entering.

On the Brink of Rebellion

As long as the procurators respected Jewish tradition and didn't tax the people too heavily, things remained relatively calm. But the people's anger toward Rome was building.

The procurators who ruled in the late 40's and in the 50's CE were especially insensitive and corrupt. Anti-Roman followers of Zadok and Judah the Galilean responded by launching a campaign of deadly tactics. Their group became known as **Sicarii,** or dagger men, because of the small curved dagger called *sicas* that they used to assassinate their enemies. Many of the Sicarii's targets were Sadducees, who were hated as traitors for cooperating with Rome.

Tensions between the rich and the poor also increased. The poor despised the rich; the rich feared the poor. Desperate Jewish bandits began raiding the farms of wealthy landowners. The Land of Israel was ready to explode.

The Revolt Begins

The procurator Florus lit the fuse in 66 CE.

Concerned with gaining ever greater amounts of gold and silver, Florus robbed the Temple treasury. When outraged Jews

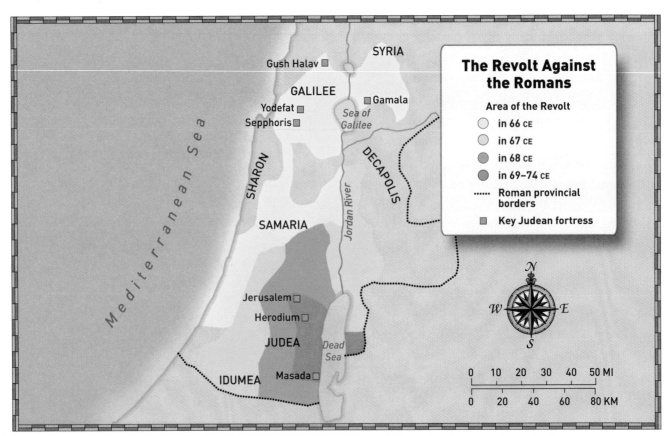

After the war against Rome, it would be almost two thousand years before the Jews would again have a national state.

protested, Florus ordered his soldiers to attack them and loot Jerusalem. The soldiers broke into homes and robbed the protesters, destroyed the marketplace, and slaughtered hundreds, including women and children.

Did Florus want a war? Oddly, yes. War would give him a reason to pronounce Jerusalem a conquered city and seize the Temple treasury. Florus got what he wanted, for by now even the Sadducees and more moderate Pharisees were swept up in the wave of anti-Roman fury. The Temple priests declared that they no longer would make a daily sacrifice in honor of Caesar, nor would they ask God to protect the Roman Empire. That was as good as a declaration of war.

War

This would have been the perfect time for Jews to unite against their common enemy. Instead, the conflicts among the various Jewish parties ripped them apart.

At first, the priests and aristocrats controlled the war. But the Sicarii soon besieged Jerusalem, declaring their leader, Menaḥem, to be the Messiah. They tried to gain control of the revolt by murdering aristocrats and looting their homes. When the Sadducees killed the Sicarii leader, the Sicarii fled to Masada, the mountaintop fortress that Herod had built in the Judean desert. There they stayed until the end of the war, praying for God to destroy their enemies, Roman and Jewish alike.

Meanwhile, on the battlefield, Jewish fighters won an early victory over Roman troops sent from Syria to restore order. But the Jewish war

As a general, Josephus was sent to the Galilee to unite and lead the population. The people were divided. On one side were the residents of wealthy cities such as Sepphoris, who believed that a war would bring ruin. On the other were bandit groups made up of the poor. They had no trust in Josephus or in the war leaders in Jerusalem, who mostly came from wealthy families.

effort was doomed. When the Roman legions under the command of Vespasian attacked in the spring of 67 CE, Jewish resistance quickly collapsed due to infighting. Joseph ben Matityahu, the general in charge, was captured and Rome took control of the Galilee. After his capture, Joseph ben Matityahu became known by his Roman name, Josephus Flavius, and he turned against the war.

Jew Against Jew

In 68 CE the Roman emperor, Nero, was assassinated. The war came to a temporary halt as Rome was overwhelmed by an internal struggle for control of the empire.

Did the Jews use this opportunity to make peace or even to organize their troops, fortify Jerusalem, and store up supplies? No. Poor farmers, laborers, and bandits who had been driven out of the Galilee now gathered in Jerusalem and formed a group called the **Zealots**. The Zealots attacked the chief priests and aristocrats—Jews—who were running the war. Soon, others who also despised the rich and powerful of Jerusalem joined the Zealots.

As if this were not enough, the Zealots and the other groups turned on one another. Jerusalem became a battlefield as Jew slaughtered Jew. Leaders of the Pharisees and Sadducees urged the people to end the civil war. No one listened.

The Fall of Jerusalem

The Romans must have watched in amazement as civil war brought their enemies to the edge of self-destruction. In 69 CE, Vespasian was made emperor. He sent his son Titus to complete the military action he had begun.

By the spring of 70 CE, Titus and his army had Jerusalem under siege. Famine quickly

These Roman soldiers were members of a special force of bodyguards that served Roman emperors. Titus was a chief officer in the guard before becoming emperor in 79 CE, upon the death of his father.

This is a model of Jerusalem as it appeared in 70 CE, just before the destruction of the Second Temple. The part of the Temple known as the Holy of Holies is in the foreground.

overwhelmed the city. The surviving factions tried to fight off the Roman invaders, but Roman battering rams cracked the walls of the city.

For the next three weeks, the priests fought bravely to keep the Romans out of the Beit Hamikdash. As the fighting raged on the ninth day of Av, a Roman soldier threw a blazing piece of wood into the Temple sanctuary. Flames shot into the air. The Beit Hamikdash burned into the next day, until there was nothing left but cinder and ashes.

Mourning for Jerusalem: Tisha B'Av

Centuries after Jerusalem's fall and the Temple's destruction, we continue to mourn our loss.

Tisha B'Av, the ninth of Av, which falls in the summer, is a day of mourning. For a full twenty-five hours, from sundown to nightfall, it is a Jewish tradition to fast. It is not a fast of atonement. Rather, it is a fast of grieving. The Book of Lamentations, which was written after the destruction of the First Temple, is chanted mournfully in the synagogue, like an ancient ballad telling a tale of love and loss. For the twenty-five hours of this holy day, Jews are prohibited from wearing leather and listening to music. Those prohibitions, too, are signs of mourning.

Why do you think the Jewish people continue to mourn the destruction of the Temple?

_____

_____

The observance of Tisha B'Av connects Jewish religious observance with our history. Describe how another holiday links religious observance with Jewish history.

_____

_____

Jerusalem and the Temple were destroyed. The surviving leaders of the different Jewish factions were led to Rome in chains. Taken with them were the sacred Temple vessels, captured as spoils of war. Jewish tradition teaches that the underlying cause of Jerusalem's destruction was not the Romans but rather the disunity among the Jews and their senseless hatred, *sinat ḥinam,* for one another. Had the Jews been unified, they might have saved the Temple.

Last Stand at Masada

Now, only isolated pockets of rebels held out against the Romans. The most serious was the Sicarii stronghold of Masada, which held large stockpiles of food and water. What the Sicarri lacked, though, was a defense against Roman technology. The Romans built a ramp up the western side of the mountain, pushed a siege tower up to the fortress, and battered down the walls. Rather than risk being taken to Rome as prisoners, most of the Sicarii committed suicide.

Earlier generations than ours often imagined the Jews on Masada as brave fighters and heroes because they refused to give in to the Romans. But, perhaps, they are better seen as symbols of why the Jewish revolt was a failure. The Sicarii were not brave warriors, but extremists who refused to fight alongside other Jews because they despised them as much as they hated the Romans. Almost until the end, the Sicarii were convinced that they were right and everyone else was wrong, that they would usher in the End of Days while all their enemies would be destroyed.

Instead of triumph, the Jewish rebellion was completely crushed. After less than one hundred years of independence, the Jews lost their country and their capital city. They watched their beloved Temple burn to the ground. But all was not lost. How the Jews saved themselves and their religion is the subject of the next chapter.

Masada is located on the top of an isolated rock, at the edge of the Judean Desert. It is the perfect place to build a fortress, high above attacking enemies who have no place to shelter themselves.

then & NOW

You have seen how, in ancient times, *sinat ḥinam,* senseless hatred, led to civil war and contributed to the destruction of Jerusalem and the loss of our homeland. Unfortunately, we have not always learned the lessons of those who came before us. For example, in 1995 Yitzḥak Rabin, the prime minister of Israel, was working to establish peace between Israel and its Arab neighbors. Jews around the world were filled with hope. But on November 4, 1995, Yigal Amir, an Israeli Jew who opposed the peace process, assassinated Rabin.

1. Is it possible to treat people with respect even if you don't always agree with what they say or do? Why or why not?

Yes because you may not have ALL differences.

2. How can following Hillel's teaching, "What is hateful to you, do not do to others," help us avoid the consequences of *sinat ḥinam?*

If you are nice and not mean, people will not hate you for no reason.

3. Describe two dos and don'ts that can guide you when expressing disagreement with others.

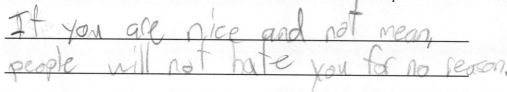

Do ___talk it out.___

Do ___once they prove you wrong or you prove them wrong, don't keep arguing.___

Don't ___fight.___

Don't ___ignore them.___

Chapter 4 Rabbinic Judaism
Learning to Reinvent Ourselves

investigate

- Could the Jews remain a united people in the Diaspora?

- How could Judaism survive without its most essential ritual, Temple sacrifice?

- In modern times, how can we continue to maintain and strengthen our Jewish identities in the Diaspora?

Key Words and Places

Ascetics	Academy
T'shuvah	Halachah
Rabbi	Synagogue
Yavneh	Beitar
Religious Court	Palestine

The BIG Picture

Imagine that you are a marine biologist. You love the ocean and have dedicated your life to studying it. Then, for reasons beyond your control, you and most of your coworkers and friends are forced to move to the mountains, thousands of miles away, never to return to the ocean or the work you love.

How might you feel? How would you begin to rebuild your life and identity? How would you maintain your relationships with your friends?

Now imagine the heartache the people of Judea felt after the destruction of Jerusalem and the Temple. For over a thousand years, with only one short interruption, the Temple had been at the heart of Jewish spiritual, commercial, and political life. Temple sacrifice was an essential way the Jews communicated with God; business was conducted in the Temple courtyards; and the Temple priests provided leadership.

Now God's home among the people had been destroyed. All that was essential to their belief system and way of life was ripped from them. Or was it?

about 68 CE	about 85 CE	about 100 CE	about 105 CE
Yohanan ben Zakkai and other rabbis gather in Yavneh; set up religious court	Religious leadership passes to Gamaliel II after Yohanan ben Zakkai's death	Rabbis at Yavneh create new prayer services for Jewish holidays	**World History:** Paper invented in China

Too Difficult to Bear

After the Jewish revolt was crushed, many Jews found the bloodshed and loss of the Temple almost too difficult to bear. A poet named Baruch expressed the misery that many felt. He looked at the rich harvests around him and felt angry that nature went undisturbed while his whole life lay shattered: "Woe unto us, for we have witnessed the suffering of Zion and see what has happened to Jerusalem…. Earth, how can you give forth the fruit of your harvest? Hold back your life-giving crops!" (2 Baruch 10:7, 9).

117 CE

Hadrian becomes emperor of Rome

132 CE

Bar Kochba leads massive Jewish revolt

135 CE

Romans defeat Jewish revolt; Bar Kochba dies

The Arch of Titus is in Rome, Italy. The arch was built after Titus's death in 81 CE to commemorate the Roman conquest of Jerusalem. The sculptured detail from the arch (see above) shows the Romans carrying off spoils of war from Jerusalem, including the Temple's branched candlestick. Why do you think the Romans included an image of the candlestick in the monument to their victory?

Coping with Tragedy

Tisha B'Av (the holiday that commemorates the day on which the Temple was destroyed) and Yom Hashoah (Holocaust Remembrance Day) are the two saddest days of the Jewish calendar. Separated by almost two thousand years, the tragic events they commemorate are the worst tragedies to befall the Jewish people. Both the destruction of the Temple and the Holocaust, during which six million Jews were murdered, threatened the survival of the Jews. Both tested the faith of those who survived.

Why do we continue to remember and commemorate these sad events?

_____

_____

_____

The emblem of the modern State of Israel includes two olive branches as symbols of peace, and the branched candlestick from the ancient Temple. Why do you think the candlestick was included in the emblem even though the Temple no longer stands?

Some responded to their overwhelming grief by becoming **ascetics**. Ascetics live a simple life, giving up pleasures, such as tasty foods, beautiful clothing, and comfortable beds. The ascetics of Baruch's time devoted themselves completely to prayer and religious study. Some chose this path as a form of *t'shuvah*, or repentance, for sins.

Why did Jews feel the need to repent? Many saw the destruction of the Temple as God's punishment. They reasoned that God was all-powerful and could not be defeated by Israel's enemies. Therefore, the only explanation for Rome's victory was that Israel must have sinned. Baruch agreed. He scolded the Jews for being disloyal to God and disregarding the wisdom of Torah. Had they followed God's teachings, he said, they would have lived in peace forever.

The Rabbis Respond

Most of the great scholars, or learned teachers, of the time were Pharisees or descendants of Pharisees. They called one another *rabbi,* meaning "my teacher." These rabbis agreed with Baruch that the Jews must accept some responsibility for the Temple's destruction. Instead of uniting, they had allowed hatred for one another to tear them apart. However, the rabbis discouraged the Jews from falling into deep despair.

Rabbi Yohanan ben Zakkai offered Jews a hopeful vision of the future, one that provided new ways to fulfill ancient traditions. One day, he and Rabbi Joshua were walking past the ruins of the Temple. "Woe unto us," Rabbi Joshua cried, "that this, the place where the sins of Israel were atoned for, is in ruins!"

Escape from Jerusalem

During the Roman siege of Jerusalem, Yohanan ben Zakkai realized that the city was doomed. Thousands of Jews were being killed, and thousands more were starving. Rabbi Yohanan wanted to leave Jerusalem so that he could save his people. But the Zealots, Jewish rebels who controlled the city gates, permitted no one to leave and surrender to the Romans. According to legend, Rabbi Yohanan pretended to be dead and had his students smuggle him out in a coffin. The Zealots had no choice but to let them out through the gates, for it was forbidden to bury the dead within the city walls.

While many of his friends remained in Jerusalem to fight to the bitter end, Rabbi Yohanan made practical plans for a future without the Temple.

Do you think Rabbi Yohanan was a coward or a hero for leaving Jerusalem? Why?

_____

_____

"My son," Rabbi Yohanan said to him, "do not be distressed. We can ask for forgiveness for our sins in another way that is as effective as [Temple] sacrifice. What is it? It is acts of loving-kindness. As the Bible says, 'God desires mercy, not sacrifice'" (*Avot de Rabbi Nathan* 6).

Yohanan ben Zakkai's response was almost shocking. Remember, many Jews believed that their ability to be close to God was destroyed with the Temple; it was only in the Temple that they were permitted to make sacrifices to God.

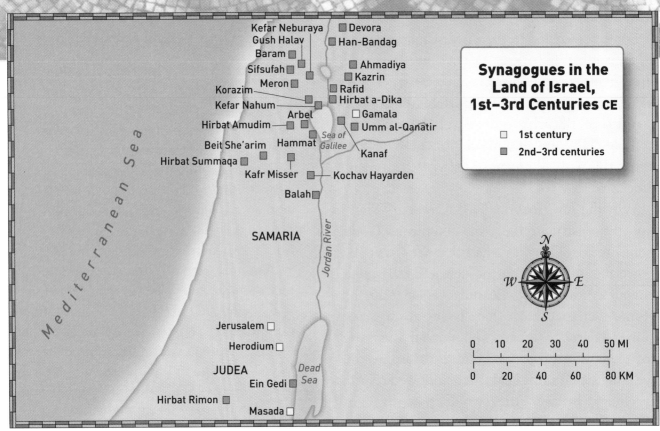

This map shows where archaeologists have found the remains of ancient synagogues.

But Rabbi Yoḥanan taught that Judaism was not tied to a particular building or to sacrifices. Instead, it was tied to the Torah, which the Jews still had and could take with them everywhere.

Yoḥanan ben Zakkai and other rabbis gathered in a town called **Yavneh,** where they set up a **religious court**. They also established an **academy,** where scholars and the best students could study, debate, and pass on Jewish teachings from one generation to the next. These rabbis never gave up their hope that the Holy Temple would be rebuilt and the rituals of sacrifice reestablished. But they also continued to develop Jewish law, or **halachah,** to meet the needs of the community. In fact, the ancient rabbis spent much of their time studying Torah, debating, and making Jewish law.

Yavneh quickly became known as the city of learned teachers and rabbis. After Yoḥanan ben Zakkai died, leadership passed to Hillel's great-grandson, Gamaliel II. Gamaliel was often addressed by the title *Rabban*, meaning "our teacher." Rabban Gamaliel and other rabbis created new prayer services for Jewish holidays, including parts of the Passover haggadah. The religious court officially decided which books would be included in the Bible, or *Tanach*. It also established official times for prayer. Rabban Gamaliel recognized that eventually prayer would become the main form of Jewish worship. Such wisdom helped Judaism survive and evolve into the religion we practice today.

Both in the Diaspora and in the Land of Israel, the role of the **synagogue** grew in

Prayer House Plus

Even before the Temple was destroyed, synagogues could be found in some Jewish communities. After the destruction of the Temple, the number of synagogues grew and their use as prayer houses became more important. This made it possible for Jews everywhere to join their community in worship.

In the space below, create an illustrated flyer that describes your synagogue.

Imagine distributing the flyer in a Judean marketplace. What would the Jews in ancient times be familiar with, based on their synagogue experience? What might they be unfamilar with that you would need to explain in detail?

Familiar _____

_____

Unfamiliar _____

_____

importance. *Synagogue* is a Greek word meaning "congregation." Many early synagogues were a combination of prayer house, Jewish community center, and guest house. Synagogues held communal prayers and Torah readings. Some also housed social activities, held classes for adults, and offered overnight accommodations for travelers.

Unlike today, in those days rabbis had no official roles in synagogues. Synagogues were under the control of local presidents, boards of directors, and prayer leaders. Some adopted practices that the rabbis would have opposed, including permitting women to serve as presidents of the congregation and decorating synagogue floors with signs of the zodiac and images of human beings and Greek gods. Scholars suggest that the Judaism practiced in these synagogues may have been quite different from the rabbis' religious teachings and rulings.

A Second Revolt

The Jewish people had shown remarkable determination and creativity. Both rabbis and synagogue leaders had succeeded in adapting Judaism to meet the needs of their changing circumstances. Yet many Jews refused to give up hope that the Temple would be rebuilt. And they still dreamed of independence from Roman authority.

In 117 CE, Hadrian became emperor of Rome. At first the Jews rejoiced because they thought he would let them rebuild their city. Instead, he announced plans to rebuild Jerusalem as a Greek-style city and he banned circumcision.

Soon after, Judea once again exploded into rebellion. Beginning in 132 CE, a leader named Simon ben Kozeva led a massive Jewish revolt. Some people, like Rabbi Akiva, believed ben Kozeva was the long-awaited Messiah. According to tradition, the coming of the Messiah would be announced by a bright star or comet, and so Ben Kozeva's supporters nicknamed him Bar Kochba, meaning "the son of a star." (Most people continued to call him Ben Kozeva—as he called himself. Yet, today, he is generally known as Bar Kochba.)

But not everyone saw Bar Kochba as a savior, nor were all Jews ready to serve in his army. Some viewed Bar Kochba as a bully and feared the consequences of his hopeless revolt. Bar Kochba responded harshly to such people, especially to those who sought safety in other towns. In a letter to the leaders of Ein Gedi, he said, "Concerning all the men of Tekoa who are found in your place—the houses in which they live shall be burned and you, too, shall be punished."

The Bar Kochba Revolt caught the Romans by surprise. Bar Kochba and his army had the same advantage the Maccabees had enjoyed—a detailed knowledge of Judea. They hid in underground caves, slipped out to perform daring raids on enemy positions, then vanished back into the countryside. Although the rebels never captured any cities, they established an independent Jewish government in the Judean hills.

Disastrous Results

Bar Kochba battled for three years. But his army was not strong enough to defeat the Romans, who had the most powerful military in the world. Hadrian sent his most experienced general to Judea. He and his army dealt mercilessly with the Jewish people. Countless villages were destroyed and many civilians were killed.

Bar Kochba and his men made their last stand in a village called **Beitar,** southwest of Jerusalem. The Romans successfully laid siege

Babata

A Jewish woman named Babata lived in the time of the Bar Kochba rebellion. In 1961, the archaeologist Yigal Yadin discovered many of her personal and legal papyrus documents in one of the Bar Kochba caves in the Judean desert. Scholars used to think she was hiding from the Romans, but today many think she was hiding from Bar Kochba, who was merciless to Jews whom he believed were not actively supporting his cause.

Babata's documents—thirty-five in all—form the largest group of ancient documents ever found in Israel. They are important because they shed light on the customs and way of life of that time. They show that Babata was married and widowed twice, participated in the business and legal affairs of her stepdaughter, Shalomzion, and was involved in several lawsuits. Just as they do today, the suits dragged on for years.

Babata's documents also included deeds to her property and her k'tubot, or marriage contracts. Similar to many k'tubot today, Babata's marriage contract protected her by stating the responsibilities of her husband. "If I [Babata's husband] die before you, you will live in my house and receive maintenance from it and from my possessions," states Babata's marriage contract.

Centuries from now, what might people learn about twenty-first-century Jewish religious school students based on your documents, such as letters, e-mails, and notebooks?

They would think we just were very old because they would have new technology

The tradition of the ketubah continues to this day. A ketubah provides written proof of when and where a couple's religious marriage ceremony was performed. In addition, it traditionally records the groom's promises to care for his bride. Many couples also include the brides' commitments.

This silver coin with a Hebrew inscription and a lyre—a harplike instrument—was issued by Simon Bar Kochba in about 134 CE.

the Galilee, to towns and villages that had not been ravaged by the war. Here, rabbis began building a new future.

Fortunately, the many adaptations to the new circumstances that had arisen after the destruction of the Temple now helped Jews face the future. Synagogues and schools were being built, and Jews were encouraged to worship God through Torah study, prayer, and acts of loving-kindness. The Jews had not only survived dark and uncertain times with courage and creativity, they had also developed new ways of thinking about and practicing their religion.

to the town and slaughtered rebels and villagers alike. Bar Kochba was killed. According to tradition, the fall of Beitar occurred on the ninth of Av (Tisha B'Av), the same day as the destruction of the Temple.

Jewish Life Ends in Judea

Hadrian treated the surviving Jews harshly. He rebuilt Jerusalem as a Greek city, banning Jews from entering its gates except on Tisha B'Av. He forbade the Jews of Judea from observing some of their most basic religious laws and customs, including the public reading of the Torah and the observance of Shabbat. Hadrian also tried to erase the Jewish nature of the land by renaming the entire Land of Israel "Palaestina," or **Palestine,** after the Philistines.

As a result of the war, the Jewish population of Judea was dramatically reduced. Some Jews had been killed, others had been captured, and yet others fled in search of safety. After more than one thousand years, Jewish life in Judea was over. The center of Jewish life, including the religious court at Yavneh, moved north to

Hadrian probably did not realize that his policies would create so much hostility. He had built many Greek cities throughout his empire, and his law against circumcision was not directed solely at the Jews. In keeping with Greek tradition, Hadrian simply believed that the human body is perfect and should not be altered.

Just as many of our ancestors could not imagine Judaism surviving the destruction of the Beit Hamikdash, so, today, we would find it hard to imagine Jewish life without the synagogue. After all, without our synagogues, where would the Jewish community gather in prayer? In celebration of the Jewish New Year, Rosh Hashanah? In times of personal joy, such as baby namings and bar and bat mitzvah celebrations?

Yet Judaism not only survived the destruction of the Temple, it flourished. It evolved to meet our ancestors' needs and it continued to evolve to meet the needs of later generations. In fact, many Jewish traditions that we take for granted as existing since ancient times are actually adaptations and innovations. For example, bar mitzvah celebrations did not exist until the Middle Ages, long after the destruction of the Temple, and women were not ordained as rabbis until a few decades ago.

1. Describe a Jewish value you share with Rabbi Yoḥanan ben Zakkai.

_____

2. Describe how you might use a modern technology, such as a computer or car, to put that value into action in a way that would not have been possible in ancient times.

_____

_____

_____

Chapter 5 Judaism and Christianity

The Parting of the Ways

investigate

- How is Christianity related to Judaism?

- Why did the conflict among the Jews and between the two religions lead to disaster?

- What can we do today to improve those relationships?

Key Words and Places

Baptism	Old Testament
Mikveh	Jewish-Christians
Resurrected	Gospels
Christians	Bishops
Epistles	Dioceses
New Testament	Pope

The BIG Picture

Roman rule over Judea was a time of great change and turmoil. It included Herod's reign, the building of the Second Temple, conflict between the Pharisees and Sadducees, two major Jewish rebellions, and, finally, the destruction of the Second Temple. If there had been newspapers in Judea, these stories would surely have made the headlines. But one story that might not even have been reported was the story of a Jew named Jesus.

Now, two thousand years later, you cannot hope to understand Jewish history without knowing the story of Jesus. That is because his life and teachings led to the birth of a new religion called Christianity, which changed the course of not only Jewish history but also world history.

about 4 BCE	about 26 CE	about 33 CE	about 50 CE	60–90 CE
Jesus born	John the Baptist preached and baptized his followers	Jesus arrested and crucified by Roman governor of Judea	Paul begins to teach his interpretation of Christian beliefs	Gospels written

A Longing for Change

To begin the story we must go back in time to the early part of the first century CE, before the two Jewish rebellions against Rome and the destruction of the Second Temple. Discouraged by foreign rule, Jews in the Land of Israel longed for political freedom. Some dreamed of a return to the golden age of King David. Many believed that Roman rule would be swept away and replaced by an age of peace and plenty. People who claimed to be messiahs, prophets, and revolutionaries often attracted large followings.

One Jew who gained attention was a man named Yoḥanan, known to history as John the Baptist. Like an ancient Hebrew prophet, John reprimanded the Jews for disregarding God's teachings. He warned that the End of Days, when all people would be judged by God, was near and that sinners would not be permitted to enter God's kingdom.

John created a new ritual, which became known as **baptism**. Baptism was based on the Jewish purification ritual of *mikveh*, which required that a person dunk his or her entire body in water. John taught that repentance purifies people of their sins and that baptism is an outward sign of that purification. Even today, some Jews wash themselves in a *mikveh* on certain occasions, such as after they have touched a dead body.

about 73 CE

79 CE

300's CE

Some Christians develop belief that Christianity is meant to replace Judaism

World History: Mount Vesuvius erupts; first detailed eyewitness account recorded of a volcano erupting

Christianity becomes official religion of the Roman Empire

51

Jesus of Nazareth

One of John's followers was a young man named Jesus, who had grown up in Nazareth, a small town in the Galilee. After he was baptized, Jesus became a traveling preacher. Like John, he urged people to repent for their sins. In addition, he spoke out against greed and injustice to the poor.

This mosaic—art made of small pieces of colored stone or glass—comes from the city of Sepphoris, which was less than four miles from where Jesus grew up.

What little we know about the life of Jesus comes from stories that were written after his death. Jesus began traveling and preaching when he was around thirty. Like stories of many religious leaders of his time, those about Jesus describe miracles he performed, such as healing the sick, changing water into wine, and walking on water. Soon Jesus had a following. Some accepted him as a prophet, in the tradition of Elijah. Others thought that he was the long-awaited Messiah.

According to Christian tradition, Jesus made a bold decision in about 33 CE. He took his message beyond the rural parts of the Galilee, straight to the center of Jewish life, Jerusalem. Jesus and his followers arrived in Jerusalem in the weeks before the festival of Passover, along with thousands of holiday pilgrims.

Arrest and Execution

Jesus spoke to large crowds at the Temple. Like the great Jewish prophets, he was critical of rich and powerful figures, accusing them of corruption and of making large donations to the Temple while ignoring the poor. He also spoke against the corruption of the priests, whom he blamed for cooperating with the Romans. One day, as Jesus neared the outer area of the Temple, he began overturning the stalls and tables of the merchants who sold birds for Temple sacrifice and the money changers who sold Roman coins.

The High Priest Caiaphas and other Jewish leaders were angered by Jesus's criticism and hostile actions. They also worried about the possibility of riots breaking out. The city streets were already packed with people preparing for Passover, a festival celebrating freedom from oppression. Jesus could easily arouse them to rebel against the Romans, whom many saw as modern-day oppressors.

The Roman governor of Judea was Pontius Pilate, a man who used brutal tactics to crush even the hint of rebellion. Caiaphas and the other priests worried about what might happen if Jesus's teachings stirred up the pilgrims. Pilate might respond by setting his troops loose on

This bronze coin from about 31 CE might have been used by Pontius Pilate or Jesus. The central image on the coin is a palm tree. Many date palms still grow in Israel today.

Jewish tradition. The main difference between this new community and other Jews was its belief in Jesus as the Messiah. This community became known as **Christians,** from the Greek word *christos*, which means "messiah" and is the source of the name "Christ." Early Christians continued to follow Jewish laws and to sacrifice at the Temple.

At first it was possible to be both Christian and Jewish. But eventually a complete break developed between Judaism and Christianity.

them, creating a bloodbath. Indeed, the historian Josephus, who lived in the first century, reported that thousands of Jewish rebels and bandits were crucified by the Romans.

According to tradition, Jesus was arrested and handed over to Pilate, who condemned him to death and executed him by crucifixion.

From Jesus to Christ

This was the end of Jesus's life—but just the beginning of his importance in history. His execution surely devastated his supporters. They may have sought comfort in the Jewish belief that God can restore people to life. Indeed, shortly after his death, some followers reported seeing Jesus **resurrected,** or raised from the dead. His supporters came to believe that Jesus was not only an earthly king but also a spiritual king and that the End of Days would soon arrive.

Over time, Jesus's followers began to identify themselves as a separate community within the

The Church of the Holy Sepulchre in Jersualem is an especially holy place for most Christians. According to Christian tradition, it is built on the ground where Jesus was crucified. Many Christians also believe that the tomb where Jesus was buried is in the church.

Seeking New Followers

In the first century, Jews often tried to persuade people to convert to Judaism, usually without success. The concept of monotheism and the close-knit nature of Jewish communities appealed to many non-Jews. But few were interested in following Judaism's restrictive laws. For example, they were resistant to following the laws of *kashrut*, which limit the foods one can eat.

Around 50 CE, a Jew named Paul began to teach that gentiles need not convert to Judaism or follow Jewish law in order to become Christians. Belief that Jesus died for one's sins and the performance of Christian rituals, such as baptism, were enough. This attracted many people. However, the Christian leaders in Jerusalem, including Peter and Jesus's brother James, opposed some of Paul's more extreme teachings. In opposition to them, Peter and James instructed Paul's converts to obey the Torah, including the laws of *kashrut* and male circumcision.

Paul pressed forward, seeking new followers in the Diaspora. He founded and supported Christian communities in cities throughout the eastern Mediterranean. Aside from visits to these communities, letters, or **epistles,** were Paul's main means of communication. He used epistles to educate the new Christians. Years later, the epistles became the earliest books to be included in the Christian sacred writings, or **New Testament**. Christians believe that the New Testament reflects a new covenant with God. They also accept the books of the Hebrew

This stairway leads to a theater in Ephesus, Turkey, where Paul preached. He may have walked these very steps.

Bible, which Christians refer to as the **Old Testament**.

As Christianity spread, it became a patchwork of communities with differing entrance requirements and views on whether or not they had to observe the laws of the Torah. Communities even differed on basic questions such as the significance of Jesus, the meaning of his death, and reports of his rising from the dead. Under the influence of some pagan religions, which had traditions related to the death and rebirth of their gods, many Christians of non-Jewish origin came to believe that Jesus was divine. They believed that he literally was the son of God.

Breaking Away

The Great Revolt (66–73 CE) confronted **Jewish-Christians**—Jews who had accepted Christian teachings—with the same question all Jews faced. Why did God permit the destruction of the Temple? Jewish-Christians came to believe that God was punishing the Jews for rejecting Jesus as the promised Messiah. Christian beliefs and practices, they said, were meant to replace Judaism.

The Bar Kochba Rebellion further distanced Christians from the Jewish community. Christians already had a messiah, so they were not interested in joining Bar Kochba. In addition, after the revolts Christians may also have seen that there were few advantages to maintaining their Jewish identities. Roman-Jewish relations had hit a low point. Jews throughout the empire were forced to pay a special tax, and the Roman government no longer recognized the authority of Judea's Jewish leaders.

The Jewish community was in crisis. Without a Temple and effective leadership, the Jews were persecuted by the ruling Romans. Early Christians were also persecuted by the Romans and didn't want to increase their suffering by identifying with the Jews. An association with the despised Jewish community would also interfere with their missionary efforts among the pagans. Over time, many Christians began to think of themselves as members of a separate religion. Others, however, continued to identify with Jews and Judaism until as late as the fourth or fifth century.

Shifting Blame

Christian communities began to gather and edit Jesus's sayings and stories about his life, creating books called the **Gospels**. *Gospel* means "good news." Christians considered the stories about Jesus to be good news, since they told about the coming of the Messiah.

The authors of the Gospels lived in a world dominated by Roman power. They did not want to offend Roman leaders. So, they shifted

Christian tradition teaches that Jesus miraculously fed thousands of his followers with only five loaves of bread and two fish. The Church of the Multiplication of the Loaves and the Fishes in the Galilee was built on the site where this miracle is said to have happened. This mosaic from the church shows the fish and a basket of bread.

Jesus of Nazareth

The exact day and month of Jesus's birth are not known, nor is there certainty about the year in which he was born. Historians believe that Jesus was probably born sometime around 4 BCE. His Hebrew name is Yehoshua, which in the Galilee may have been pronounced as "Yeshua."

The Gospels do not provide much information about Jesus's youth. However, they do say he was circumcised and that he was interested in Jewish religious teachings. After he was baptized, Jesus traveled throughout the Land of Israel, particularly in the Galilee, preaching to large crowds that often included laborers, fishermen, and other people of simple means. He emphasized the importance of justice and compassion, and offered hope of a better world, a coming "Kingdom of God" on earth to those who suffered.

In what ways were Jesus's teachings similar to those of the Hebrew prophets?

_____

_____

_____

_____

Some of Jesus's most dedicated followers, such as Peter, James, and Paul, traveled widely, teaching the Gospels and seeking new followers.

A Scene from the Gospels

Pontius Pilate was known to be a cruel Roman governor. Yet, in the Gospels, a story is told in which he agrees to set one Jew free from prison, as a goodwill gesture toward the Jews at their holiday time. The crowd chooses to release a bandit rather than Jesus.

Pilate asks the crowd, "What should I do with Jesus who is called the Christ?" The crowd responds, "Let him be crucified!" *The Gospel According to Matthew* describes Pilate symbolically washing his hands before the crowd, declaring, "I am innocent of his blood." The crowd responds, "Let his blood be on us and let it be on our children!"

Some people today still believe that the Jews were responsible for Jesus's death. How would you explain to such a person your understanding of what happened?

_____

_____

_____

_____

_____

_____

the blame for Jesus's crucifixion away from the Romans and toward the Jews. The Gospels were interpreted as teaching that Jews not only denied that Jesus was the Messiah, but were also guilty of his murder. As Christianity and Judaism became separate religions, sections of the Gospels became the basis of misunderstanding and hatred.

It is important to remember, however, that the Gospels were written *before* Christianity had split from Judaism and that most of the authors were Jewish. These authors debated as brothers and sisters with the Pharisees and other survivors of the First Revolt. Together they questioned what the life and death of Jesus and the destruction of the Temple meant. True, some of the arguments were vicious, but so, too, can family arguments be emotionally charged, as are some arguments among today's Jews. The tragedy is not that insults were hurled but that after Christianity split from Judaism, the understanding of the times in which this family feud took place was forgotten.

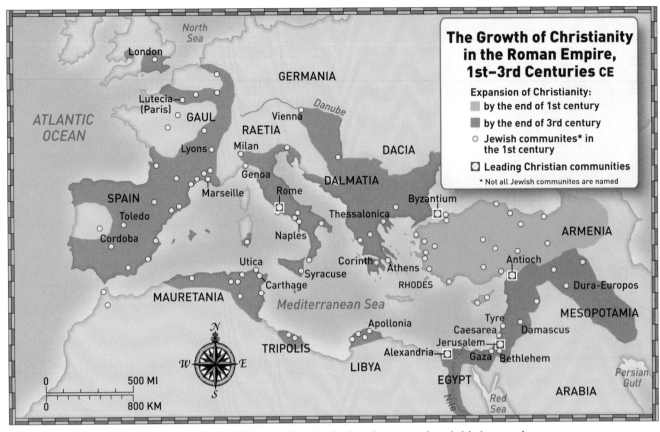

The Growth of Christianity in the Roman Empire, 1st–3rd Centuries CE

Expansion of Christianity:
- by the end of 1st century
- by the end of 3rd century
- Jewish communites* in the 1st century
- Leading Christian communities

* Not all Jewish communites are named

Christianity spread quickly throughout the Roman Empire during the second and third centuries.

Christianity's Growing Influence

Christian leaders were not the only ones who were critical of their rivals. Rabbis hurled insults at Christians and sought to limit their growth and influence. But rabbis had little power under the Roman rule. In contrast, Christianity was spreading quickly and gaining influence. By the fourth century, three hundred years after Jesus, Christianity became the official religion of the Roman Empire.

The Christianization of the Roman Empire greatly deepened the wedge that had built up between Christianity and Judaism. Now Christian leaders were able to use the power of Rome to enforce their prejudices. By the fifth century Jews were officially denied many of their traditional rights and privileges, including the right to build new synagogues, hold state office, and serve in the army.

The wedge grew even greater as both religions became more centralized. Christian leaders called **bishops** were recognized as religious authorities and determined the proper practices and religious guidelines for their **dioceses,** or regions. The chief bishop, who headed the diocese in Rome, became known as the **pope**.

Judaism, too, became more centralized. Banned from participating in many of the public activities of the Christianized Roman

Christians and Jews Living in Peace

Today's political ads sometimes distort the degree to which a community or country is divided. So, too, our understanding of ancient history would be distorted if our knowledge were limited to what we know about the religious leadership. In fact, although Jewish and Christian leaders were often in conflict, many Jews and Christians interacted peacefully.

Before the Christianization of the Roman Empire, Jews, Christians, and pagans interacted freely in the Galilee and in many Diaspora communities. Even in the fourth and fifth centuries churches, synagogues, and pagan temples existed side by side in urban centers, including Rome. Some Christians even worshipped with Jews in their synagogues.

The Rise of Christianity and Its Split with Judaism

- The Romans oppress the Jews; dejected, many Jews yearn for liberation through a messiah.

- John the Baptist criticizes the Jews for their sins and offers forgiveness through baptism.

- Jesus is baptized, begins to preach, and develops a following.

- Jewish leaders are concerned that, in reaction to Jesus and his followers, Pontius Pilate will unleash troops in Jerusalem.

- Jesus is crucified; reports of his resurrection inspire faith in him as the Messiah.

- Jesus's followers identify themselves as a separate community within the Jewish tradition; the main difference is their belief in Jesus as the Messiah.

- Around 50 CE, Paul teaches that gentiles can become Christians without converting to Judaism; he begins to found Christian communities throughout the eastern Mediterranean.

- By 90 CE, some Christian communities develop the belief that Christianity is meant to replace Judaism.

- By the fourth century CE, Christianity becomes the official religion of the Roman Empire.

- Both Judaism and Christianity become more centralized.

Empire, Jews were forced to turn inward. Local synagogues and Jewish communities increasingly became the centers of Jewish life. As a result, community elders, synagogue leaders, and rabbis grew in their influence and power.

This is how Judaism and Christianity eventually split into two separate religions and why centuries of hostility between Christians and Jews followed. Once the seeds of hatred and misunderstanding had been planted, they mushroomed into repeated acts of violence. The consequences were tragic and became a central theme in Jewish history.

Yad Vashem is the Holocaust memorial in Jerusalem. It includes a tree-lined path called the Avenue of the Righteous, a memorial to non-Jews who risked their lives to save Jews. What are some of the beliefs and values these non-Jews may have in common with our own community?

then & NOW

As you have learned, Christianity's roots are in Judaism. In the beginning, the differences between Jesus's teachings and those of other Jewish preachers were not great. Despite the increased differences that developed, there is much that Judaism and Christianity still have in common: Both revere not only the Torah but also the books of Prophets and Writings as sacred. And both instruct their followers to love and honor God, pursue peace and justice, and perform acts of loving-kindness.

1. How might teaching non-Jews about Judaism add peace to the world?

    _____

    _____

    _____

2. What would you most want to teach others about Judaism? Why?

    _____

    _____

    _____

3. What would you most like to learn about another religion? (Be specific.) What action can you take to become more knowledgeable?

    _____

    _____

    _____

Chapter 6 Babylonia
The New Center of Jewish Life

investigate

- What challenges did our ancestors face?

- How did they adapt to life in Babylonia?

- In what ways did they provide a model for strengthening the twenty-first-century Diaspora?

Key Words and Names

Oral Law	Geonim (Gaon)
Mishnah	Islam
Gemara	Koran
Talmud	State-Sponsored Religion
Palestinian Talmud	
Babylonian Talmud	Muslims
Biblical Judaism	Mosques
Rabbinic Judaism	Karaites
Exilarch	Heretics

The BIG Picture

Hoping to find freedom and opportunity, people who suffer from persecution or poverty sometimes leave their country and settle in a new land. Such shifts in population have occurred many times in Jewish history.

After the disastrous Bar Kochba Rebellion, as Christianity spread throughout the Roman Empire, large numbers of Jews left Judea in hopes of a better life. Many moved north to the Galilee or went to Syria and other parts of the Hellenistic world. But others traveled east to Babylonia, where Jews had lived for generations, after the destruction of the First Temple.

Jewish life in the Galilee eventually weakened because of the intolerance of the Roman Empire's Christian rulers. As the Galilee declined, Babylonia continued to grow more powerful. For over five hundred years, Babylonia served as the center of Jewish learning and growth. During this period, the Jews found new ways to enrich Jewish tradition and values as they adapted to and prospered in their new country.

about 200	about 400	about 500	570
Mishnah completed	Palestinian Talmud completed	Babylonian Talmud completed	Muhammad, prophet of Islam, born in Mecca

Collecting the Law

After the Bar Kochba Rebellion, small Jewish communities survived in Judea—now renamed Palestine by the Romans. Rabbi Judah the Prince was one of the many rabbis who remained in ancient Palestine. He dedicated his life to developing a standardized oral record of Jewish law. Much of it was based on **oral law**—legal rulings that had been passed on by word of mouth from one generation to the next. In about 200 CE, Rabbi Judah and his students completed this collection. It became known as the **Mishnah**. The Mishnah was a revolutionary work. Its legal rulings allowed Judaism to adapt to the reality of life without a Temple.

about 600	638	642	711	882
World History: Chaturanga, an ancestor of chess, first played in India	Jerusalem captured and placed under Muslim control	Babylonia, a center of Jewish life, captured and placed under Muslim control	Spain, a center of Jewish life, captured and placed under Muslim control	Saadiah ben Joseph (Saadiah Gaon) born in Egypt; becomes great scholar

Next Step: The Talmud

The Jewish population of Babylonia had declined after the rebuilding of the Temple when Jewish leaders returned to Israel. Now, after the destruction of the Second Temple, the Babylonian Jewish community was growing. Jews lived, worked, and worshipped in peace. Scholars traveled from Palestine—where they had learned the rabbinic tradition—to Babylonia, bringing their teachings with them. In 219, the Babylonian sage Rav, who had spent years studying in Palestine with Rabbi Judah the Prince, returned to Babylon. The Talmud recounts that when Rav returned to Babylon, "we became like the Land of Israel." The rabbis of Babylonia and their students discussed the Mishnah with great excitement.

Meanwhile, similar conversations were going on in Tiberias and other rabbinic centers in the Galilee. Many of these discussions are recorded in the **Gemara**. The Gemara is a compilation of discussions of Jewish law, interpretations of the Bible, parables, stories, traditions, and folklore. Much of it is written in Aramaic, the language of Babylonia. Unlike the Mishnah, which makes little direct reference to the Torah, the Gemara often refers to the Torah to support its opinions. Together, the Mishnah and Gemara make up the **Talmud,** meaning "study" or "learning."

Two versions of the Talmud were compiled, one in the Galilee and the other in Babylonia. The **Palestinian Talmud** was completed in the Galilee around 400 CE, while the **Babylonian Talmud** continued to be expanded and edited into the sixth century.

The Palestinian Talmud was written in haste because the chaos in the Roman Empire and the growing intolerance for Jews caused the communities in the Galilee to decline. Interestingly, the Talmud produced in the Diaspora of Babylonia became far more influential in Jewish life. Where the two Talmuds disagree on a matter of Jewish law, the Babylonian Talmud is generally followed.

The Talmud and its commentaries fill thousands of pages. Its largest volumes deal with the issues of day-to-day living. For example, there are laws concerning property rights, the obligations of employers and employees, and which foods to eat and which to avoid. There are also laws that discuss how to observe special occasions, such as Shabbat and holidays.

As a guide to Jewish living, the Talmud helps adapt Jewish law to life in the Diaspora. For example, it calls for Jews to follow the laws of the country they live in. So long as the king acts

These are the remains of a Talmudic village in the Golan Heights, north of the Sea of Galilee.

Each page of the Talmud has a clear structure. The Talmud text is placed in the middle, surrounded by the commentaries of later generations.

fairly, the Talmud declares, "the law of the land is the law."

Before the Talmud, **biblical Judaism** had been the foundation of Jewish life. The most influential leaders of biblical Judaism were the Temple High Priests. Many of them were Sadducees. In contrast to the Sadducees, the Pharisees were in a good position to lead the community after the Temple's destruction, for they had emphasized the importance of studying and interpreting Jewish law over performing Temple rituals. Many Jews were resistant to accepting rabbinic law. But **rabbinic Judaism,** which was based on the Talmud, slowly became the foundation of Jewish life. It continues to be the basis of Judaism to this day. Learned Jews still study the Talmud and the commentaries that have been written on it over the centuries.

A Land of Opportunity

Rabbis from the Land of Israel who traveled to Babylonia were astonished by its agricultural wealth. It was a fertile land and many Jews became successful farmers. Others worked in business and trade. Some Jewish traders traveled as far as China to buy or trade for silk. Others processed the silk for sale. There were also Jewish bankers, Jewish tax collectors, Jewish soldiers, and even a Jewish elephant rider.

While living under the rule of the Babylonians, the Jews separated

What Do You Think?

The Talmud teaches, "A father is obligated to perform a *brit milah* on his son, to redeem him [from his commitment to serve in the Holy Temple], to teach him Torah, to arrange for his marriage, to teach him to earn a living.... Rabbi Judah says: Whoever does not teach his son to earn a living, teaches him to become a criminal. A criminal—can you truly mean that? It means that it is *as though* the father taught his son to become a criminal" (Tractate *Kiddushin*).

Do you agree with Rabbi Judah? Why? What other obligations should parents have to their children? What obligations should children have to their parents? Why?

Arriving in a New Land

Imagine making the journey from the Land of Israel, which had been devastated by war, to the fertile land of Babylonia. What might you find exciting about this new land? Why?

_____

_____

What might your concerns be about leaving the Land of Israel? Why?

_____

_____

Now return to modern times. How might the challenges your family faced in coming to this country have been like the challenges the Babylonian Jews faced? How might they have been different?

Same Challenges   **Different Challenges**

_____   _____

_____   _____

_____   _____

political and religious authority within their own community, just as they had in the days of the kings, prophets, and Temple priests. Their political leader was called the **exilarch,** meaning "head of the Jewish community of the exile." The exilarch's primary duty was to settle conflicts between the Jewish community and the Babylonian government. The exilarch was also responsible for collecting taxes and appointing judges in the Jewish community.

The heads of the great Jewish academies in Babylonia provided religious leadership. These rabbis were known as **geonim** (pronounced gue'onim; singular, gaon), literally meaning "geniuses" and "learned." The geonim were great scholars of the Talmud. However, we know very little about the daily life of Babylonia's Jewish community and the extent to which Jews accepted rabbinic Judaism and the leadership of the geonim.

The Challenge of Islam

In the first half of the seventh century, Arab armies swept out of Arabia and conquered most lands where Jews were living. The armies brought with them a new religion called **Islam,** meaning "submission to God." The founder and central prophet of this new faith was Muhammad. Muhammad was raised in the Arabian city of Mecca, where he lived among both Jews and Christians. There he came to believe in one God. He warned of a coming day of judgment and declared himself the last and greatest of the prophets. Muhammad introduced a new holy book. It became known as the **Koran,** the holy book of Islam.

Muhammad and his successors waged war against their neighbors. They achieved spectacular success, capturing Jerusalem in 638, Babylonia in 642, and much of Spain in 711. All the great centers of Jewish life were now under Islamic rule. This meant that Islam was the **state-sponsored religion,** or official religion, in those parts. Other religions could be practiced only to the extent permitted by the **Muslims,** or followers of Islam.

In Babylonia and elsewhere, Muslims usually granted the Jews the right to practice their religion without interference. In fact, Islam recognized both Jews and Christians as "people of the book" (the Bible), or monotheists, and granted them protected status. But as protected non-Muslims, Jews had secondary status. For example, they had to stand aside when

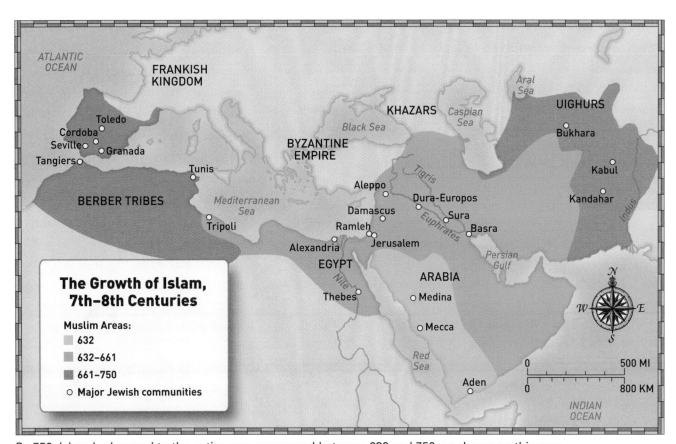

By 750, Islam had spread to the entire area conquered between 632 and 750, as shown on this map.

This manuscript illustrates the Muslim army's siege of the city of Messina in Sicily, which it captured in 843.

The Roots of Islam

For Muslims, acceptance of Muhammad's teachings includes acceptance of Allah as the one God, God as the source of sacred texts (including the Bible), and the importance of the prophets (including Moses and Jesus). Because Muhammad recognized the influence of other monotheistic religions on his teachings, at first he did not consider what he preached to be a new religion. Instead, he expected Jews and Christians to accept his ideas as additions to their traditions. But they did not. So Muhammad emphasized the differences.

Muhammad instructed his followers to turn away from Jerusalem when they prayed and to turn instead toward Mecca. He made Friday the day of holy assembly and, in contrast to Judaism and Christianity, work was permitted on that day. Most of Judaism's dietary laws were rejected, although a few continued to be observed, such as not eating pork.

Yet, to this day, there are shared traditions. Many stories in the Koran originated in the Bible, such as stories about Abraham. Numerous Jewish teachings and ethical sayings are included in the Muslim tradition. And, among the holy places of Islam are the tomb of Abraham in Hebron and the burial site of John the Baptist's head in the Great Mosque of Damascus.

passed by a Muslim in the street. Synagogues had to be smaller than neighboring **mosques,** or Muslim houses of worship. Jews were encouraged to convert to Islam (which some did), but Muslims were forbidden to convert to Judaism. Still, for centuries Jews enjoyed greater freedom under Islam than under Christianity.

The rise of Islam created additional challenges for the Jews of the Middle East, including Babylonia. First, Islam made Arabic the primary language of their world. Less educated Jews, who knew Arabic but not Hebrew and Aramaic, found themselves cut off from Judaism's most important texts. In addition, the Arabs developed new forms of scholarship, including grammar, philosophy, science, medicine, and commentaries on texts. The traditional Jewish focus on law suddenly seemed insufficient in a world that valued more diverse knowledge and skills.

Jews in Babylonia were determined to meet these challenges. They produced Jewish books in Arabic and Judeo-Arabic, Arabic words written in Hebrew letters. Under the influence of their neighbors, they also explored new fields of study, creating commentaries, grammars, and philosophic works of their own. Many of these works blended traditional Jewish teachings with Arabic teachings. They made it possible for Jews who might otherwise have completely assimilated, or abandoned their Judaism in favor of the Babylonian culture, to live in both worlds. Furthermore, they enriched not only Jewish culture, but also the larger, general culture.

The Karaite Challenge

Diaspora Jews were challenged not only by Islam. They were also challenged by Jews who, influenced by Islam, followed only what the Torah says, not the words of the rabbis. These Jews denied the authority of the Talmud, the exilarch, and the geonim. While challenges to

The Dome of the Rock in Jerusalem is the oldest Islamic building to survive in its original form. It is one of Islam's holiest sites. Muslims believe that it is the place from where Muhammad rose to heaven. It was built over the site of the Second Temple.

Just as we are influenced by the people and culture around us, so, too, were the Babylonian Jews. Arab culture helped them create new forms of Jewish scholarship, which in turn strengthened their Jewish identities.

Saadiah Gaon

Saadiah ben Joseph (882–942) was the greatest of the geonim. Born in Egypt, he studied in both Israel and Babylonia before becoming the gaon of the Babylonian academy of Sura.

Saadiah, also known as Saadiah Gaon, translated the Bible into Arabic and produced a prayer book with Arabic instructions and explanations. He wrote the first Hebrew grammar book, a Hebrew dictionary, and Hebrew poetry. Because Greek philosophy was valued by many educated and assimilated Jews in the Arab world, Saadiah wrote (in Arabic) *The Book of Beliefs and Opinions*. In it he showed how one could believe in both the Torah and the teachings of Greek philosophers.

Most earlier geonim had focused on the Talmud and Jewish law. Saadiah showed that Jews could take what they learned from the surrounding culture—language, philosophy, values, and more—and adapt it in ways that strengthen Judaism. He proved that Judaism could not only survive but also thrive in the Diaspora.

Describe a way in which you, or your family, have combined Jewish tradition with other traditions. For example, you might decorate your sukkah with maize, in synagogue sing Adon Olam to the tune of "Deep in the Heart of Texas," or collect tzedakah to help your town's library.

_____

_____

_____

_____

Just as the sages read and studied from the Torah, so, too, does each new bar and bat mitzvah learn to carry on Jewish tradition. By discussing the Torah's text, we honor the tradition of helping everyone understand its lessons.

Life in Babylonia presented the Jews with many challenges and opportunities.

CHALLENGE	ADAPTION
It was difficult to pass on the oral tradition now that the Jews were dispersed.	Record the oral tradition in the Mishnah.
There was a need to translate the general principles of the Mishnah into practical laws to guide real-life situations.	Develop the Gemara and additional commentaries.
Jews spoke Arabic, which became the main language in Babylonia after the Islamic conquest. Many forgot Hebrew.	Translate the Bible and prayer book into Arabic and develop the language of Judeo-Arabic.
Secular society valued diverse knowledge and skills.	Broaden Jewish studies to include subjects such as philosophy, Hebrew grammar, and commentary on texts.
There were temptations to assimilate.	Focus Jews on Judaism's strengths.
Some saw a conflict between the law of the land and Judaism.	Declare that as long as the civil laws are just, Jews must honor them.

rabbinic authority dated back to the time of the Temple, the new challengers were particularly noteworthy. The large size of their movement, the fact that their views seemed in tune with the general Islamic culture, and the distinguished reputation of the man they considered their founder gave them special standing.

Anan ben David was a person of great learning and piety, and it was said that he was a descendant of King David. According to some, he was in line to be appointed exilarch in the eighth century, but was passed over because of his uncompromising and strict ways. Respected as a scholar and righteous man, Anan ben David soon became the guiding light for a group called Ananites. Following his death, he also became the guiding light for a Jewish sect,

known as **Karaites**. The Karaites insisted that the Bible alone is the source of God's law.

Following a statement in Psalms, the Karaites declared that "the Torah of Adonai is perfect" and does not need to be interpreted in order to be understood. Their views brought them in conflict with the rabbis. For example, the rabbis permitted Jews to keep a fire burning throughout Shabbat, so long as it was lit beforehand. In contrast, taking the biblical commandment to kindle no fire on the Sabbath day literally, the Karaites ruled that their followers must spend Shabbat without fire for light and heat.

Karaites also refused to follow the traditional Jewish calendar set by the rabbis. Applying the literal words of the Torah, they declared that the holiday of Shavuot must always fall on a

Sunday. In addition, based on the teachings of the prophets, the Karaites favored elaborate mourning rites for the destruction of the Temple and the exile of the Jewish people from the Promised Land. Some of their synagogues resembled mosques and—like Muslims—they removed their shoes before entering them.

The geonim considered the Karaites **heretics,** people who violated accepted Jewish teachings and rulings. The rabbis defended rabbinic tradition and sought to undermine the basis of Karaite beliefs. For centuries, however, mainstream Jews and Karaites continued to interact and to marry one another, for each considered the other part of the Jewish people. Over time, though, the two communities grew farther apart, much as we have seen that early Jews and Christians did. They became separated by differences in belief and practice that proved too great to bridge. By the sixteenth century, the rabbis decreed that Jews could not marry Karaites. Today, the Karaite community consists of about thirty-five thousand people, most of whom live in Israel.

Beyond Babylonia

The influence of the geonim and the Talmud grew in Muslim countries, such as Egypt and North Africa. It especially grew in Spain, which had a strong economy. Jewish communities were also growing in parts of Christian-controlled Europe, including France and Germany. These centers of Jewish life drew scholars and rabbis away from Babylonia. The Talmud, which had been written in Babylonia, was soon being studied in Jewish communities in Europe, Asia, and Africa. It enabled Jews in diverse Diaspora communities to discuss and observe the same set of laws

The Babylonian model of Diaspora life, however, continued to be highly influential. Living as a minority in a non-Jewish environment, Jews had learned how to adapt their lives to their new surroundings and how to renew Jewish life.

Jews such as Albert Einstein, Steven Spielberg, and Ruth Bader Ginsburg have made significant contributions to the larger worlds of science, entertainment, and law, even as they maintained their Jewish identities. In 1996, U.S. Supreme Court Justice Ginsburg wrote, "I am a judge born, raised, and proud of being a Jew."

then & NOW

Jews under the Greek influence of Hellenistic culture translated the Torah into Greek, and Jews under Arab influence in Babylonia translated the Bible into Arabic. So, too, in North America, we have translated our Jewish texts into English.

Like our ancestors, the North American Diaspora has adapted to changing circumstances in a number of ways. Influenced by the feminist movement, the Reform, Reconstructionist, and Conservative movements began to ordain female rabbis in the late twentieth century. To help families who may not know how to conduct a Passover seder, religious schools now offer model seders. And many synagogues and Jewish Community Centers (JCCs) offer courses in Bible study, prayer, modern Hebrew, and CPR.

1. List one adaptation the Babylonian Jewish community made and describe what you think might have happened had it not been made. Explain why you think so.

_____

_____

_____

_____

2. List one question your community should consider before changing an established custom or before creating a new one. Explain why.

_____

_____

_____

Chapter 7

Sepharad and Ashkenaz

Judaism's Growing Diversity

investigate

- In what ways did the Jewish communities of Spain and Germany differ?
- What challenges did they face?
- How did their choices help create the diversity of today's Jewish world?

Key Words and Places

Sepharad	Ashkenaz
Golden Age of Spain	Moneylenders
Nagid	*Parnasim*
Jewish Mystics	*Kahal*
Kabbalah	Excommunicated
Zohar	*Tosafists*
Mishneh Torah	Ḥasidei Ashkenaz

The BIG Picture

Just as many Jews left Judea in search of a better life, so, centuries later, many left Babylonia. In time, two new centers of Jewish life developed in areas that are known today as Spain and Germany.

Today you can travel from Spain to Germany in about the time it takes to play a baseball game. But a thousand years ago, there were no jets, railroads, or automobiles. People didn't often make the nine-hundred-mile trip because it was long and difficult. There were also no televisions, telephones, or computers to help communicate the latest news, fashions, recipes, and court rulings.

As a result, the Jews of Spain and of Germany developed in different ways. Each was influenced by the surrounding culture and its non-Jewish population, especially its attitudes toward Jews. As always, the Jews adapted to the world around them and, in the process, Judaism became more diverse and enriched.

711	950	993	about 1000
Muslim armies cross Straits of Gibraltar into Spain; soon conquer most of country	Golden Age of Spain begins; lasts about 200 years	Samuel Hanagid born in Spain; becomes scholar, rabbi, and military commander	**World History:** Gunpowder invented in China; used in fireworks and weapons

The Golden Age of Spain

In the year 711, Muslim armies, originating in Arabia and North Africa, crossed the Straits of Gibraltar into Spain. Within four years most of the Iberian Peninsula (modern-day Spain and Portugal) was under Muslim rule. As a result, Spain became religiously and culturally diverse: Muslims ruled; Christians were tolerated; Jews, being neither Christian nor Muslim, served as valuable intermediaries, or go-betweens. People of different ethnic and cultural backgrounds, Middle Easterners and Europeans alike, came to know one another and work together.

Spain prospered under Islam. Cities grew and Spain became a land of opportunity, a crossroad for international trade. Jewish immigration into Spain—or **Sepharad,** as it was called by the Jews—swelled. It quickly developed into a leading center of Jewish learning and culture. In fact, this period in Jewish history is known as the **Golden Age of Spain.**

1040	1135	1286
Rabbi Solomon ben Isaac (Rashi) born in France; becomes biblical and Talmudic scholar	Moses Maimonides (Rambam) born in Spain; becomes scholar and writes Mishneh Torah	Moses de Leon writes *The Zohar,* the basic textbook of the Kabbalah

As these pages from the Koran demonstrate, Islamic art includes patterning, geometric design, and calligraphy, which is the art of beautiful handwriting.

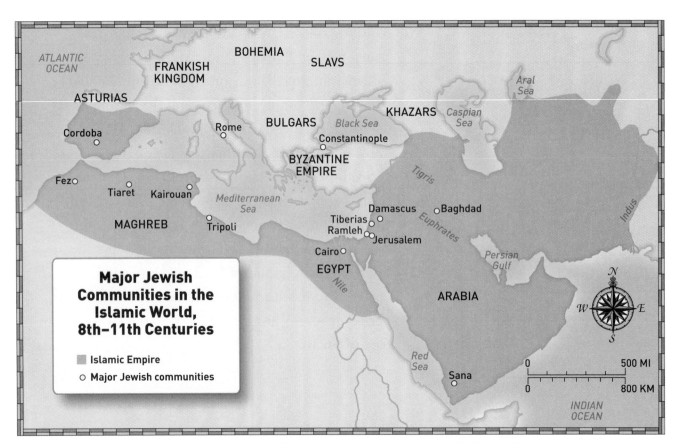

Major Jewish Communities in the Islamic World, 8th–11th Centuries

- ■ Islamic Empire
- ○ Major Jewish communities

As the Islamic Empire grew, thousands of Jews immigrated to the west, especially from what is now Iraq and Iran. Strong ties were developed between the western Jews of Sepharad and those who remained in the eastern countries.

The Golden Age began in the middle of the tenth century and lasted about two hundred years. Inspired by Muslim poets, Jews began writing beautiful poetry in both Hebrew and Arabic. Jews also made contributions to the study of philosophy, medicine, science, Bible commentary, Jewish law, music, dance, and the visual arts.

Samuel Hanagid was born Samuel ibn Nagrel'a in 993. *Nagid* means "head of the Jewish community." Considered one of the most influential Jews of his time, he was both a great secular and Jewish scholar, and a brilliant

Living in Two Worlds

While there may not be many people as talented as Samuel Hanagid, in modern times there have been many Jews who, like him, have been active in both the secular and Jewish worlds. Belle Moskowitz (1877–1933) was a close adviser to New York's Governor Alfred E. Smith and a powerful figure in the Democratic Party. She was the most prominent Jewish woman in politics in her day. She was also a social worker and a leader of the National Council of Jewish Women.

Describe one activity in which you participate in the secular world and one in the Jewish world.

Secular: _____

Jewish: _____

Sound Familiar?

Sharing Cultures

Jews interacted regularly with Muslims and Christians in their daily lives and at work. They learned to combine Jewish tradition with the exciting mix of cultures that surrounded them. For example, Arabic poetry influenced Jewish literature and the Jews learned to cook kosher foods that were influenced by Spanish recipes and spices.

Such cultural sharing is a common theme in Jewish history. Describe an instance when a friend or neighbor from a different ethnic or religious background influenced you—perhaps broadening your taste in foods or the sports you enjoy—by teaching you about his or her culture.

_____

_____

_____

Describe one way you may have influenced a non-Jew by teaching him or her about Judaism and Jewish culture.

_____

_____

_____

_____

A Poet and a Scholar

Although education was rare among women of this time, there were exceptions. Qasmunah, a poet from a leading Spanish Jewish family, was one such woman. Unfortunately, only three of her short poems were preserved. All three were written in Arabic.

Another highly educated woman was the daughter of a community leader in Baghdad who gave lessons in Torah and Talmud. A scholar who taught men, she went to great lengths to conduct herself with modesty. According to Rabbi Petachia of Ratisbon, who visited the Jewish community of Baghdad, her modesty led her to teach male students through a window. "She herself is inside the building, while her students are below, outside, and do not see her."

Sometimes we simultaneously participate in the secular and Jewish worlds. For example, we do so when we use the Internet to access information on Jewish history and traditions, and when we observe the mitzvah of tzedakah by contributing to a local hospital, animal shelter, or public library.

statesman, poet, rabbi, and military commander. In fact, he became the vizier, or commander, of the city of Granada and spent eighteen years in command of a largely Muslim army. He also wrote three books of poetry, commentaries on the Bible, and a major work dealing with Jewish law.

Judah Halevi, who lived from 1075 to 1141, was also a shining star during the Golden Age of Spain. In addition to being the greatest of Spain's Jewish poets—some eight hundred of his poems are still studied to this day—he was also a leading philosopher, physician, and merchant. As a young man, he wrote secular poetry and lived a carefree life. But when he was about fifty years old, he turned his back on this easygoing life and dedicated himself to his faith in God. He often wrote of his desire to settle in the Land of Israel. Eventually, he did travel east, first to Egypt and then to Palestine, where he died two months after he arrived.

Judah Halevi believed that the Jewish people were distinguished by their closeness to God, sacred language, tradition, and worship. This view of Judaism had a strong influence on **Jewish mystics,** Jews who rejected the idea that God was unknowable.

The teachings of the mystics became known as the **Kabbalah.** In addition to study, mystics used fasts, chants, and meditations in an attempt to glimpse the secrets of God's world. They thought that human beings could interact with angels and work to counter the forces of evil.

In Spain in 1286, Moses de Leon wrote the *Zohar,* or "Book of Splendor." Written partly in Hebrew and partly in Aramaic, it became the basic textbook of the Kabbalah. It offers "hidden" mystical explanations of selected biblical words and verses. For example, the letters of a word might be scrambled to uncover a new meaning in a passage. Followers of Kabbalah believed that by discovering such hidden meanings, we can learn much about God, the creation of the world, God's relationship to human beings, and good and evil.

Students of Kabbalah still read the *Zohar* today. But, just as many Jews in our time are not mystics, so, too, during the Golden Age of Spain, not all Spanish Jews were mystics. Some Jews even considered efforts to uncover the secrets of God's world to be dangerous. In fact, there is a tradition that mysticism should be seriously explored only by scholars who are at least forty years old.

The most learned and famous Spanish-born Jew was Moses Maimonides, also known as the Rambam. Maimonides criticized the mystics for insisting that Judaism was full of secrets. Instead, he taught that Judaism is essentially a religion of reason. He believed that, like philosophy and science, Judaism makes sense when you study and think about it. Maimonides wrote the first complete code, or detailed summary, of Jewish law, a fourteen-volume work known as the **Mishneh Torah**.

A Jewish Frontier Land

While Sephardic Jewry was flourishing, important centers of Jewish life were also developing in northern France and western Germany. Jews called these areas **Ashkenaz,** based on the Hebrew word for Germany. Small Jewish communities had existed in this part of Europe since the time of the Roman Empire, when Jews came as sailors, traders, and craftspeople. As time went on, Jews also became shopkeepers, tailors, peddlers, butchers, poets, and doctors. In addition, some Jews became **moneylenders**. (Christians needed non-Christians to serve as their moneylenders because their religious law forbade them to charge interest on loans made to other Christians.)

This fourteenth-century illuminated manuscript is from the second section of Maimonides's Mishneh Torah. It includes the laws of the Sh'ma and Amidah. At the top of the page is a quote from the Book of Psalms 119:97. It begins: "How I love Your Torah."

Maimonides

Maimonides was born in Cordoba, Spain, in 1135 but, as a result of religious persecution, he and his family fled Spain, settling in Egypt. Gifted, Maimonides became the court physician to the vizier of Egypt. But medicine was only one of several interests Maimonides had. He was also a great rabbi, author, philosopher, and community leader.

Moses Maimonides

As Saadiah Gaon had done in Babylonia, Maimonides helped the Jews of Spain understand how they could adapt to the surrounding culture in ways that strengthened Judaism. He wrote *The Guide of the Perplexed* in which he sought to teach the "science of [Jewish] Law." In it he tried to demonstrate how Judaism was compatible with the study of science. For example, he taught that the laws of *kashrut* have both physical and spiritual purposes. He said that the foods forbidden by the Torah are all unhealthy in some way. In addition to his Jewish books, Maimonides wrote medical guides on everything from surviving snake bites to maintaining a healthy lifestyle.

Describe why Maimonides is a model for living a committed Jewish life while also being active in the larger culture.

_____

_____

_____

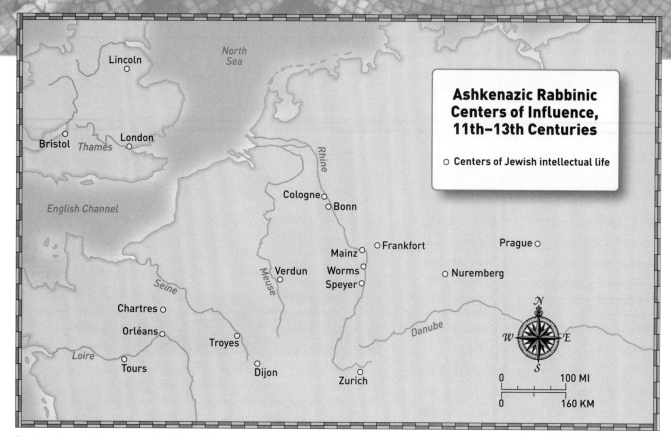

By the eleventh century, thriving Ashkenazic Jewish communities, such as Troyes, Mainz, and Worms, had become centers of Jewish learning and trade.

The Jewish population of Ashkenaz was modest in comparison to those of Spain and the Middle East. According to the Jewish traveler Benjamin of Tudela, only 6,000 Jews lived in the six largest French communities. Germany's Jewish population was no more than 20,000. But the Ashkenazic population grew steadily until the fourteenth century. By 1300 there may have been as many as 100,000 Jews in France alone.

In many communities, the rights, privileges, and obligations of Jews were spelled out in detailed legal charters. Under the terms of these charters, Ashkenazic Jews largely governed themselves. The church, which had a strong influence in secular matters, discouraged the kind of social and cultural relationships that Jews and Muslims had built in Spain.

Reynette of Koblenz: Moneylender

By the thirteenth century, there were married and widowed Jewish women who had become successful money-lenders in European countries such as England, France, Germany, and Spain. Reynette of Koblenz was a moneylender who lived in Germany in the fourteenth century. At first she worked with her husband, Leo. Later, after she was widowed and remarried, her skills and success grew. Eventually, the size of her financial dealings exceeded those of both her husbands.

As a result, Ashkenazic Jews generally did not write religious works in the local language, nor did they pursue scientific and secular studies, as they did in Spain. The leading communities—such as Mainz and Worms in Germany, and Troyes in France—became centers of commerce where Jews and Christians traded with one another. But creative Jewish scholarship was restricted to the Hebrew language and was mostly limited to traditional Jewish texts.

Ashkenaz was a Jewish frontier land in the eleventh century. It was far from other centers of Jewish life. Communication with distant Jewish communities was infrequent and difficult. Jewish traders and merchants were the main sources of news from far away. As a result of their isolation, Ashkenazic Jews formed tight-knit communities that were less open to outside influences than those of Sepharad. In larger towns, Ashkenazic Jews often settled in the same neighborhood. Families lived within walking distance of one another, the synagogue, and other Jewish services, such as the kosher butcher.

Jewish community leaders, called ***parnasim,*** sought to develop a system of communal government, including a court system and rules about fair business practices. The *parnasim* were usually the elders of their community. Most often, they came from wealthy and leading families. Some had close ties to the secular authorities and could speak with them on behalf of the community when there was a problem. Others were respected as Torah scholars.

Eleventh-century Worms was a center of Jewish learning. Rashi was among the great scholars who studied there. The first synagogue of Worms was founded in 1034. Over the years, it has been rebuilt and remodeled several times.

In each community *parnasim* organized an independent board, called a ***kahal,*** that managed the day-to-day affairs. The *kahal* collected taxes from the community to provide for services such as schools and tzedakah for the needy. The *kahal* strictly regulated community behavior. Those who did not follow the community standards could be **excommunicated,** meaning that they were excluded from the community and shunned by its members.

The work of Gershom ben Judah, known as Rabbenu Gershom Me'or Hagolah ("light of the Diaspora"), helped to set Ashkenazic Judaism on its own course. Gershom lived in Ashkenaz from about 960 to 1028. He built an academy in Mainz that served as a training ground for Ashkenazic rabbis. He also issued a series of rulings that adapted Jewish law to the circumstances the Jews found in Ashkenaz. His most famous ruling banned polygamy—or having more than one wife. The Jews' Christian neighbors considered polygamy immoral. Gershom's ruling was a break from Jewish tradition in Muslim lands.

Rabbi Solomon ben Isaac, known as Rashi, extended the work of Rabbenu Gershom. He lived from 1040 to 1105. His academy in Troyes drew students from across Ashkenaz. Most important, Rashi produced a series of writings that offered short, clear, simple explanations of difficult words and concepts that appear in the Bible and Talmud. He also translated difficult words into French, which was spoken by French Jews. (His commentaries contain about ten thousand French words.)

In this way, Rashi made it possible for students to understand Judaism's greatest texts and thereby honor and pass on Jewish tradition. In addition, his works are filled with rulings based on Jewish law. These rulings helped the Jews of Rashi's day to live as Jews in their new European homelands.

After his death, Rashi's students continued his work. Many of them were scholars known as

Marriage Ashkenazic Style

Marriage was arranged by parents. Usually, the bride and groom came from families of the same social and economic status. Rabbenu Gershom's ruling forbidding men from marrying more than one wife originally applied only to the town of Mainz. But by the mid-twelfth century it was widely accepted in northern France, Germany, and even in England. Gershom also forbade a man from divorcing his wife without her consent.

Betrothal, or engagement, generally occurred at age eight or nine. Jewish girls typically married at age eleven or twelve and boys at about thirteen or fourteen. (In Germany and France, Christian girls typically married at twelve or thirteen, and boys were usually in their late teens or twenties.) Given the young marriage age and other stresses of life, divorce was fairly common.

tosafists, meaning "those who add." The *tosafists* contributed new commentaries on the Bible and the Talmud. Rashi's work is still studied today.

As in Spain, some Jews in Ashkenaz studied mysticism. These mystics had much in common with the ascetics who gave up life's pleasures after the destruction of the Second Temple. The mystics, too, devoted themselves to religious study and prayer as a form of repentance. Their religious observance went far beyond what Jewish law demanded and they added special prayers that, they thought, would draw them closer to God.

The mystics of Ashkenaz were known as **Ḥasidei Ashkenaz**, meaning "the pious Jews of Germany." Many of the prominent leaders were members of one extended German Jewish family, the Kalonymus family. The teachings of Ḥasidei Ashkenaz spread throughout Germany, France, and Italy.

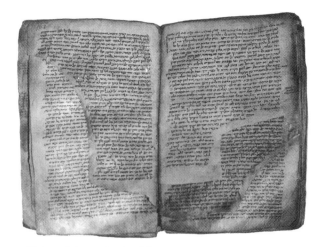

This edition of a Rashi commentary on the Later Prophets was produced in about 1250.

A Tradition of Diversity

Both Sephardic and Ashkenazic Jews remained committed to the values and traditions of Judaism. They believed in the same Torah, studied the same Talmud, celebrated the same holidays, and founded their communities upon the same rabbinic heritage. Yet their understanding and practice of Judaism differed in significant ways. The Jews of Sepharad developed a tradition that was strongly influenced by the Muslim cultural world with which they interacted. In contrast, the Jews of Ashkenaz were more isolated. They did not integrate as much of the culture that surrounded them into their observance of Judaism.

Unfortunately, one common experience that both the Sephardic and Ashkenazic Jewish communities were about to face was a sharp rise in intolerance and violence. The story of the Ashkenazic Jews is next.

Like Father, Like Daughter

Among Rashi's accomplishments was that he raised three learned daughters—Yocheved, Miriam, and Rachel. All three were Torah and Talmud scholars, and experts on *kashrut.* It is said that when her father was ill, Rachel wrote a response to a question of Talmudic law posed by Rabbi Abraham Cohen of Mayence.

then & NOW

You have learned about some of the differences between the Ashkenazic and Sephardic communities. You have also learned that, despite their differences, both continued to study the lessons of the Torah and Talmud, observe Jewish traditions and values, and identify as members of the same people.

1. Describe one similarity and one difference between yourself and one of your friends.

Similarity _____

_____

Difference _____

_____

2. How does the similarity strengthen your relationship? How does the difference enrich it?

Similarity _____

_____

Difference _____

_____

3. Describe one similarity and one difference between yourself and Jews from another community, for example, a friend's synagogue or Jews in another country. How might the Jewish people benefit from both the similarity and the difference?

Similarity _____

_____

Difference _____

_____

Chapter **8** Medieval Europe

The Rise of Religious Persecution

investigate

- What caused the violence and persecution against the Jews?

- How did the Jews respond?

- What responsibility toward others might these experiences teach us?

Key Words and Places

Infidels	Blood Libel
Crusade	Inquisition
Guilds	Disputations
Middle Ages	Black Death

The **BIG** Picture

By the eleventh century, the Ashkenazic Jewish communities were strong and well established. Christians and Jews lived side by side in relative peace. But medieval Ashkenaz was complex. Periods of calm often were shattered by outbreaks of anti-Jewish violence and persecution. The first major outbreak began in 1096, after Pope Urban II called for the liberation of the Holy Land from the Muslims.

Response to the appeal was swift and enthusiastic. The pope promised forgiveness of sins and eternal reward for those who joined in the effort. Many Christians saw this religious or holy war as a great adventure and an opportunity to gain wealth.

So began the series of wars known as the Crusades, which started with anti-Muslim feelings among the Christians but also grew to include anti-Jewish feelings. The events that followed robbed the Ashkenazic communities of their sense of security and strained Jewish-Christian relationships for centuries.

1095	1099	about 1148	1215
Pope Urban II issues call to liberate Holy Land from Muslims	Christian armies conquer Jerusalem; crusaders slaughter Muslims and Jews	First known blood libel charge in Middle Ages made in Norwich, England	Pope Innocent III requires Jews to dress differently from Christians

Warning Signals

Pope Urban II publicly challenged Christians to form armies, march to Palestine, and capture the Holy Land from the Muslims who controlled it. He referred to Muslims as **infidels,** or nonbelievers. Jews feared the Christian armies, which were heavily armed and aroused by religious fervor: in their passion the Christian armies could easily turn on the "infidels" next door—the Jews—rather than Muslims far away.

Sensing the threat, French Jews held a day of fasting and prayer for the entire Ashkenazic community. "May God save us and save you from all distress and suffering," the German Jewish leaders wrote to the Jews in France. "We deeply fear for you. However, we have less reason to fear [for ourselves] for we have not heard so much as a rumor of the **Crusade**."

1290
Jews expelled from England

about 1290
World History: Eyeglasses invented in Italy

1306
Jews expelled from France

1348–1350
Plague sweeps across Europe

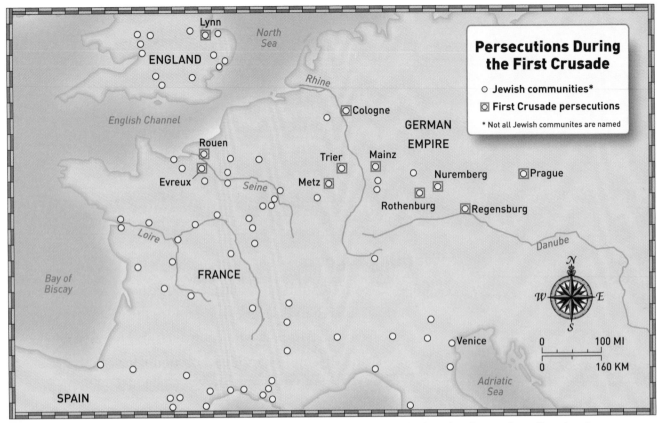

Persecutions During the First Crusade

○ Jewish communities*
◎ First Crusade persecutions

* Not all Jewish communites are named

Jewish communities in Europe were sometimes attacked and destroyed by bands of crusaders. Despite the devastation, in most cases the communities quickly rebuilt what they had lost.

Ironically, French Jewry escaped relatively unharmed. The German Jews were not as lucky. As the French crusaders swept through the Rhineland, they stirred up the local population against infidels. Disorganized, violent bands made up of the poor and the ignorant attacked the Jews, who were closer at hand than Muslims. Often they were joined by middle-class townspeople who resented the Jews as business competitors.

Violence first broke out in Speyer, where Jews were slain in the streets by an angry mob. The rest of the Jewish community was saved only by the town's bishop, who gave them refuge in his castle.

As news spread up the Rhine River to the Jewish community in Worms, panic also spread.

Pope Urban II with Peter the Hermit, a religious leader who was known as a preacher of the Crusade in France

From the eleventh to the thirteenth centuries, four major Crusades sought to capture the Holy Land from the Muslims.

Some Jews fled to the local bishop, offering him gold and jewels in return for protection; others hid in their homes. But when the violent mob reached Worms, the townspeople joined in the murderous rioting. Jews were dragged from their homes and slaughtered. The fortunate ones were given a choice: convert to Christianity or die.

Similar horrors shook the towns of Mainz and Cologne. The Jews did all they could to resist the attackers, but in the end they were overwhelmed. Thousands of Jews were murdered, and some of the most important Jewish communities in Germany were destroyed.

As terrible as the massacres of the First Crusade were, they were still isolated events. Yet, even when it appeared that life was changing for the better, the seeds of conflict continued to be sown.

Sleepy Towns No More

Europe was changing. Forested land was being cleared, roads were being built, and new technologies such as water mills and iron plows were increasing farmers' productivity. More efficient agriculture enabled people to produce more food than they needed. The surplus food could be traded for other items. Trade in everyday goods such as timber, grain, wine, metal goods, and wool expanded. Sleepy towns were transformed into lively market centers.

At first, the Jewish communities of Ashkenaz viewed these changes favorably. The bustling economy created new opportunities for Jewish merchants. Moneylenders were also becoming more important; they helped with the start-up of new businesses. Christians were taught by their religious leaders that profit-making was ungodly and that "love of money is the root of all evil." As a result, both trade and money lending were dominated by Jews.

The Crusade Reaches Palestine

The First Crusade also affected the Jews in Palestine. When the Christian armies conquered Jerusalem in 1099, crusaders slaughtered both Muslims and Jews. Under Christian control, the city was forbidden to Jews. However, large Jewish populations were still permitted to live in coastal cities.

Ironically, while the Crusades were the cause of great suffering, they also resulted in closer ties between Jews in Europe and the Holy Land. With the European Christians in charge of Palestine, it became easier to travel between Europe and Palestine. In 1267, Moses ben Naḥman, a great Spanish rabbi and Jewish legal scholar known as Naḥmanides, or Ramban, settled in Palestine. A small migration of rabbis and scholars continued even after the Muslims recaptured the land.

The Jewish people's ability to adapt to new circumstances is like a life vest. It helps us keep afloat and survive in difficult times.

Competition and Conflict

The financial rewards of trade, however, soon gained more influence with Christians than the teachings of the Church. Increasingly, Christians became merchants and Jewish merchants became their competitors. Christian merchants used their

Changes in Technology	Adaptations in Christian Society	Adaptations in Jewish Society
New technologies enabled fewer farmers to produce more food. The surplus food was traded. Small towns grew as trade increased.	Fewer people needed to live and work on small farms and in villages. Large cities developed. Money was needed to expand businesses.	Jewish communities became more city-centered. A middle class of Jewish traders developed. Jews became bankers to provide money for Christian businesses.

religion—which was the official religion of the state—to great advantage. They won the right to govern their towns without interference from kings and nobles. They set up their own **guilds,** or trade associations, which allowed them to control the quality, quantity, and price of goods. Jews were forbidden from joining the guilds or enjoying their benefits. As a result, Jews were forced out of trade.

Laws were passed that made the lives of Jews not only more difficult but also more insecure. In Germany, for example, Jews were forbidden to bear arms, a sign of honor in the **Middle Ages**—the period of Western Europe's history from the fifth to the fifteenth centuries. Many rulers stripped Jews of their freedom, legally defining Jews as royal property. Rulers then demanded large sums of money from the Jewish community in the form of special taxes. The Jews were pushed from both sides: hated as moneylenders by the general population and taken advantage of economically by kings and nobles.

Another threatening trend was the growing power of the Catholic Church. Church leaders used their increasing political influence to attack those whom they considered enemies, both at home and abroad. They also used their influence to persecute the Jews. In most cases, the Church did not encourage physical violence against the Jews, but it did not want the Jews to prosper. Its policy was based on the teachings of Saint Augustine: Jews were to be segregated from the rest of society. They were to be kept in a lowly position to serve as witnesses to the truth and wisdom of Christianity.

Church leaders preached fiery sermons against the Jews, stirring up uneducated peasants with accusations that the Jews had killed Jesus. They also repeatedly spoke of the Jewish

Money Lending: A Dangerous Profession

One profession that continued to be dominated by Jews was money lending. The reason was simple: in many places, this was the only profession legally open to Jews. At best, this was a mixed blessing. While some Jewish lenders became wealthy, social tensions increased. Christians of all classes needed loans, but felt resentment toward the people to whom they owed money. The Jews, who were restricted in their professional options by the guilds and the government, had no choice but to charge interest. That was how they could make a profit and earn a living.

The resentment that developed toward the Jews often led to prejudice and violence. Dolce of Worms (see page 92) was killed by thugs who were unable to negotiate what they considered agreeable terms for a loan. Seeing the valuables in her home, they robbed and savagely murdered Dolce and her two daughters.

Dolce of Worms

Dolce of Worms lived in twelfth-century Germany. The wife of a well-known rabbi, she earned money to help support her husband's study of Torah. Dolce lent money, spun wool, made ritual objects such as wicks for the synagogue candles, and cared for the daily needs of her husband's students who boarded with the family. She also served as a teacher and model to other women in her community. Dolce taught the women how to chant prayers and sometimes led special services for women.

Dolce's ability to provide both financial support for her family and spiritual leadership for the Jewish community inspired her husband to write these words about her after her death: "Her husband trusts her completely. She fed and clothed him in dignity so that he could take his place among the elders of the land, and offer Torah study and *mitzvot*…. She sings hymns and prayers…. In all the towns she instructed women (so they can) chant songs."

Why do you think that Judaism teaches both the value of earning a living and the value of religious observance? (Hint: See "What Do You Think" on page 65.)

_____

_____

_____

_____

Cultural Borrowing Continues

Despite competition and conflict between the Christians and Jews of Ashkenaz, the two groups lived and worked side by side in relative peace throughout most of the twelfth and thirteenth centuries. As a result of mixing socially and for business, the Jews were influenced by Christian practices. For example, many customs associated with Purim originated in Christian Germany. Traditions such as dressing up in costumes and drinking alcohol on Purim were inspired by the Catholic festival of Carnival, which was celebrated at about the same time of year with drinking, dancing, and masquerades.

Similarly, Judaism has influenced others. For example, the American Puritans based their way of life on the ideals of high moral behavior and hard work, which they learned from the Bible. In time, these ideals became American values.

What secular custom might you want to integrate into the celebration of a Jewish holiday or life-cycle event? (Name the holiday or event.) Why? How?

_____

_____

_____

What Jewish custom might you want to integrate into the celebration of a secular holiday. (Name the holiday.) Why? How?

_____

_____

_____

For many of us, dressing up in costume is a Purim tradition that starts in childhood. Some costumes are based on the story of Esther; others borrow ideas from the secular world.

connection to money lending and taught that the Jews were in league with the devil.

The Jews Are Accused

In this poisonous environment, Jews soon found themselves accused of horrendous crimes. One common charge was that Jews murdered young children and used their blood for religious rituals. The first known **blood libel,** or ritual murder charge in the Middle Ages was made by a clergyman in Norwich, England, in about 1148. He made up a story about how, in 1144, the Jews of Norwich had taken a young boy and reenacted Jesus's last hours by torturing and crucifying him. Recognizing the charge as a lie, the local sheriff protected the Jews. But the story spread from England to France and Germany, where accusations of ritual murder often set off violent anti-Jewish riots.

The Catholic Church, meanwhile, issued new orders designed to separate Christians and Jews. In 1215, Pope Innocent III required Jews to dress differently from Christians. In some communities, Jews were already distinguishable by their beards and clothing, so the pope's edict had little effect. But in the larger cities, such as Paris, Jews and Christians were almost indistinguishable. These Jews were required to wear special badges on their clothing.

In 1233 the Church set up a court known as the **Inquisition** to investigate and remove heretics—people who disagreed with Church teachings and rulings. While inquisitors mainly concerned themselves with Christian heretics, Jews were sometimes targeted. Some of the most zealous inquisitors were former Jews who had converted to Catholicism. Unlike other Church leaders, they had a deep and personal knowledge of Judaism. To prove the truth of Christianity to the general population, the former Jews challenged the rabbis to public **disputations,** or debates.

The inquisitors who had converted from Judaism were able to embarrass the Jews by pointing to passages in the Talmud that spoke ill of Christians and insulted Jesus and Mary. They also tried to use their knowledge of the Hebrew Bible to point to passages that could be interpreted as demonstrating the truth of Christianity.

Pope Innocent III called a meeting of bishops and other leaders—both religious and secular—to create a program to deal with people who disagreed with Church teachings. This meeting was known as the Fourth Lateran Council. The council also issued decrees designed to separate Christians and Jews.

The situation grew worse. In 1290, the small Jewish community of England was expelled, followed in 1306 by the expulsion of Jews from France. The royal treasuries seized all the Jewish land, houses, and other possessions. The

This painting portrays a woman who was tried by the Inquisition. One of the many lessons of the Inquisition is that intolerance often leads to oppression and violence.

order was devastating; over 100,000 Jews were forced from their homes. Some crossed the border into Germany; others sought refuge in Mediterranean countries such as Italy.

In the Grip of Terror

Then, between 1348 and 1350, a plague known as the **Black Death** swept across Europe. It was the deadliest epidemic the world had ever seen, killing twenty-five million people, or about one-third of all Europeans. A terrified population, helpless against a disease they did not understand, frantically searched for causes.

Despite the deaths of many Jews from the plague, some Europeans blamed them for

the epidemic. In the grip of terror and irrational hatred, they charged Jews with spreading the sickness by poisoning wells and rivers. Thousands of Jews were killed in riots by uncontrollable mobs.

The Talmud on Trial

Church leaders challenged rabbis to a series of public disputations. Church scholars sought in particular to discredit the Talmud. They believed that if they could discredit it, more Jews would convert to Christianity.

The Talmud itself was put on trial in a famous disputation in Paris in 1240. Over ten thousand books and scrolls were seized from synagogues throughout France. Nicholas Donin, who had converted from Judaism to Christianity, led the prosecution. Donin charged that the Talmud was a wicked collection of books that insulted Christians.

Rabbi Yeḥiel ben Joseph led the defense team. But it was hardly a fair trial—he and his colleagues were locked in separate prison cells when the hearings were not in session. No one was surprised when the Talmud was condemned and all the copies that had been seized were burned.

This painting shows Jews being burned to death for causing an outbreak of the Black Death. Years after the plague passed, scientists determined that the disease was carried by fleas living in the hair of black rats. Humans contracted the disease either by fleabites or by contact with human victims.

On the Move Again

The Jews of Ashkenaz learned a bitter lesson: they were not safe in this part of the world. Repeating the pattern of their ancestors, many families packed up their belongings and set off in search of a better life in new lands. This time Jews moved east. They flocked to the under-developed regions of Lithuania and Poland, where their skills as merchants were welcomed.

Why were many Sephardic Jews also looking for a new home at this time? That question brings our story back to Spain, where the Golden Age had come crashing to an end.

then & NOW

During the medieval period, Christians were in the majority and often had power over people of other religions. For example, Christian merchants forbade Jews to join their guilds, which had the effect of forcing Jews out of trade.

1. Describe a time when you were in a group and were in the majority. On a scale of 1 to 10, 10 indicating very powerful, how did you feel? Why?

_____

_____

_____

2. Describe a time when you have been in the minority. Using the same scale of 1 to 10, how did you feel? Why?

_____

_____

_____

3. Based on your study of Jewish history and values, do you think Jews have a special responsibility to protect the rights of minority groups? Why or why not?

_____

_____

_____

Chapter 9

The Sephardic Diaspora
Rebuilding Jewish Life

investigate

- Why were the Jews forced out of Spain?

- How did the Sephardic Jews adapt Judaism to the conditions in their new countries?

- How do we continue to be influenced by their ideas and innovations?

Key Words and Places

Conversos	Ladino
Crypto-Jews	Safed
Marranos	Tikun
Sephardic Diaspora	Shulhan Aruch
Dhimmi	

The BIG Picture

Of what world-changing event does the year 1492 remind you? Most people immediately think of Christopher Columbus setting out from Spain and sailing to the Americas. But the Jews of Spain would have a different answer. In 1492 King Ferdinand and Queen Isabella issued an order expelling "all Jews and Jewesses of whatever age they may be" from Spain. Jews were warned: Never return, even as travelers.

This was a catastrophe for the Jews of Spain. Yet they not only survived, they thrived. Facing an uncertain future with courage, creativity, and flexibility, Sephardic families spread out in many directions. They built Jewish communities from Asia to Africa to the Americas. Working together and developing new traditions, they enriched Judaism, and their contributions continue to illuminate Jewish life to this day.

1391	1455	1481	1492	1497
Thousands of Jews murdered in anti-Jewish riots in Spain	**World History:** German inventor Johann Gutenberg begins printing and selling Bibles	Spain's Catholic Church introduces Inquisition	King Ferdinand and Queen Isabella expel all Jews from Spain	Jews expelled from Portugal

Secret Jews Go Underground

Conditions in Spain had been changing for centuries. Beginning in the eleventh century, Christian armies slowly gained control of Spain from the Muslims. At first, Christian rulers were welcoming to Jews. In fact, many Jews moved from Muslim areas, which were becoming less tolerant, to areas controlled by Christians.

By the late 1300's, however, as the Catholic Church gained power in Spain, Jews faced increasing persecution. Thousands of Jews were murdered in a series of anti-Jewish riots in 1391. Thousands more saved their lives only by converting to Christianity. These Jews, known in Spanish as *conversos,* were forbidden by the Catholic Church from returning to Judaism.

1569

Isaac Luria moves to Safed; his ideas revolutionize Jewish mysticism

1665

Claim made that Shabbetai Zevi is the long-awaited "King Messiah"

1666

Shabbetai Zevi arrested by Ottoman government; converts to Islam

The Santa Maria la Blanca synagogue, in Toledo, Spain, was founded in 1180. It is the city's oldest synagogue. The structure and design were strongly influenced by Islamic architecture and art. In the fifteenth century, Christians seized the synagogue and converted it into a church.

Many *conversos* became faithful Catholics. Others went back and forth between Judaism and Catholicism. But some *conversos*, women in particular, began to practice Judaism in secret. For such Jews, no law, not even the threat of death, could cut them off from their faith and traditions. These *conversos* became **crypto-Jews,** or secret Jews. For example, they secretly lit Shabbat candles on Friday night and recited Jewish prayers only in the privacy of their homes. Often they were encouraged and aided in their underground practices by Jews who had not converted.

The Jews Are Expelled

Those suspected of being secret Jews were sometimes known by the insulting term *marranos,* a Spanish word meaning "swine." Determined to expose Jews who practiced their faith in secret, Spain's Catholic Church introduced the Inquisition in 1481. The Inquisition focused on uncovering and punishing secret Jews.

Church officials accused thousands of people of being secret Jews. The accused were arrested, questioned, and in many cases tortured. Those who repented by agreeing to abandon Judaism were punished, often by having their property confiscated. Those who refused to repent were burned at the stake.

When they saw that even the Inquisition could not stamp out Judaism in Spain, King Ferdinand and Queen Isabella issued an order expelling all Jews in 1492. Only Jews who converted to Christianity were permitted to remain. In early August 1492, just as Jews around the world observed the saddest day of the Jewish calendar, the fast of Tisha B'Av, twelve hundred years of Jewish life in Spain came to an end.

Searching for a Place to Live

Many of the Jews who left Spain settled in nearby Portugal. But in 1497 the royal families of Spain and Portugal united in marriage and Portugal's Jews were forced to convert. In a movement that came to be known as the **Sephardic Diaspora,** Jews from Spain and Portugal spread out in search of new homes.

Some traveled across the Mediterranean Sea to North Africa, Italy, and the Ottoman Empire. Others found a tolerant home in Western European states, like the Netherlands, which had rejected Catholicism for the

In 1492, the same year Christopher Columbus's three ships set forth from Spain on the voyage that led them to America, Spain expelled all Jews and warned them never to return, not even as travelers.

You Are There

Spain

Life as a Secret Jew

Imagine what it might have been like to practice Judaism in secret. You might always wonder: *Who is looking at me and questioning if I'm a secret Jew and studying Torah at home?* You would have to take many precautions in your daily life. For instance, you could not let anyone know that you are fasting on Yom Kippur. Which three Jewish traditions would you choose to honor? How would you accomplish this in secret?

1. _____

_____

2. _____

_____

3. _____

_____

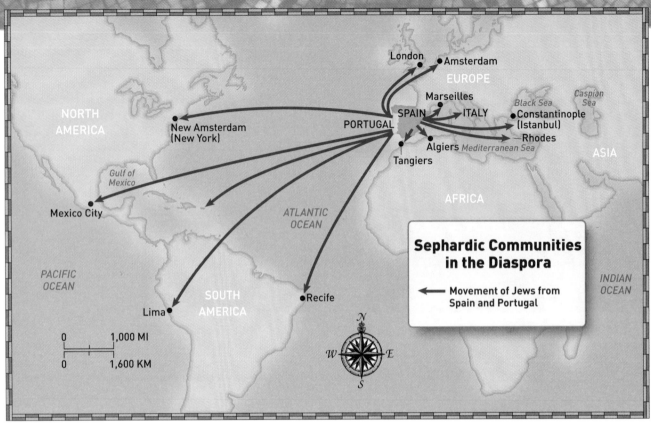

The expulsion of Jews from Spain and Portugal in the fifteenth and sixteenth centuries created an extended Sephardic Diaspora. It stretched as far east as the Ottoman Empire and as far west as the Americas.

new "Reformed Christianity" known as Protestantism. Still others made the trip across the Atlantic to newly established colonies in Central and South America that they thought lay beyond the reach of the Inquisition.

Today, when you read the newspaper or watch television, you may see images of people who have been displaced by war or ethnic conflict. Such people often have seen their homes and property destroyed or taken from them, have been tortured or imprisoned, and may have no safe place to live. The Jews of the Spanish Diaspora faced similar hardships. Many had been tortured and jailed and had their wealth taken from them, and there were

few countries that wanted to accept them. Ultimately, large numbers of Sephardic Jews settled in the Muslim-ruled Ottoman Empire, which included present-day Turkey, much of the Middle East, and Southeastern Europe.

The Ottoman emperor considered Jewish artisans, craftspeople, and merchants valuable newcomers. Under Muslim law Jews were *dhimmi,* members of a protected monotheistic, minority faith. As *dhimmi*, they were not the equals of Muslims and had to pay special taxes in return for the safeguarding of their lives and property. But at least they were permitted to enjoy a great deal of economic freedom and to practice their religion openly.

Doña Gracia Nasi

Doña Gracia Nasi, often known simply as Doña Gracia, was one of the greatest Sephardic Jews of her day. Born to a family of Spanish Jews that had been forced to convert to Christianity, she grew up in Portugal as a secret Jew. In 1542, when she was thirty-two years old, Doña Gracia took control of her family's banking and trading business.

Portrait medals, such as this one of Doña Gracia, were commissioned by rulers, church officials, and the middle-class. This is the earliest identified medal of a Jewish person that includes a Hebrew inscription. Doña Gracia's name has been inscribed in Hebrew on the left side of the coin.

Doña Gracia moved from Portugal to France to Italy—constantly on the run from rulers who were eager to prove that she was a secret Jew and then seize her fortune. Not only did she continue practicing Judaism, she also boldly used her money to help persecuted *conversos* escape from Portugal. Like many others, Doña Gracia finally settled in Turkey where she could live openly as a Jew. All her life, she continued to be an active and outspoken defender of Jewish communities. She even established a synagogue—perhaps the first Jewish woman to do so.

Why do you think Jews like Doña Gracia were willing to risk their lives to remain Jewish?

_____

_____

Ladino: A New Language of Our Own

Jews in the Ottoman Empire developed their own language, known as Ladino. A mixture of Turkish, Hebrew, and Spanish, it is the Sephardic equivalent of Yiddish, which was developed by East European Jews. Having a language of their own helped Jews maintain their common culture and distinctive way of life.

Several thousand Jews in Israel still speak Ladino, and a Ladino newspaper is published in Istanbul. Ladino music is finding new audiences today as religious and secular tunes are performed in synagogues and concert halls and distributed on CDs.

These are the members of Alhambra. They research, arrange, perform, and record music of the Jews of Sepharad, including much Ladino music. Alhambra plays many instruments that are common in the Middle East.

Rebecca Machado Phillips was born in New York in 1746 to crypto-Jews who fled Portugal. As an adult, Phillips became a wife, mother, fundraiser, and social activist. She helped raise money for ritual objects for the Mikveh Israel synagogue and was a founder of the Female Association for the Relief of Woman and Children in Reduced Circumstances.

The Long Road to New York

Seeking to escape the Inquisition, some *conversos* crossed the ocean in the mid-1500s and settled in places such as Lima, Peru, and the Portuguese colony of Brazil. While under Portuguese rule, those who practiced Judaism in secret lived dangerously. When the more tolerant Dutch captured parts of Brazil, those Jews once again were able to observe their religion openly. But in 1654, when Portugal recaptured Brazil, the Inquisition returned and Jews as well as Protestants were forced to leave.

In September 1654, twenty-three of these Jewish men, women, and children stepped off a ship in the Dutch colony of New Amsterdam, where they established the first Jewish community in North America. Just ten years later, the British captured New Amsterdam and renamed it New York. Today New York City is home to about one million Jews.

Repairing the World

Generations of Sephardic Jews struggled to make sense of their expulsion from Spain and Portugal. Some considered it a punishment from God. Others came to believe that the expulsion was part of a series of events that would lead to the coming of the Messiah and the return of all Jews to the Land of Israel.

Could Jews help bring the days of the Messiah closer? Many believed that in the Land of Israel they could. Some ten thousand Jews settled in the city of **Safed** in the Galilee. Dedicating themselves to study and prayer, they became especially devoted to the study of Kabbalah. They meditated, engaged in all-night study sessions, and prayed passionately, hoping that their intense spiritual efforts would help bring the Messiah.

The most influential religious leader in Safed was Rabbi Isaac Luria, known to his followers as "the Holy Lion," Ha'ari Hakadosh. Although he died at the age of only thirty-eight, his ideas revolutionized Jewish mysticism and even

The word tzedakah comes from the same root as the word tzedek, meaning "justice." How can giving to those in need add justice to the world and help repair it?

changed the way Jews prayed. Most important, Ha'ari introduced the idea of *tikun,* or repair. *Tikun* is the belief that through prayer, meditation, and observing *mitzvot,* or commandments, an individual can help "repair" the world, or restore it to a more perfect state. Instead of waiting for God to act, Ha'ari emphasized how much human beings might accomplish.

Following False Messiahs

Sometimes people want to believe something so badly that their judgment becomes clouded. Have you ever so wanted to believe that school would be canceled because of a forecasted snowstorm that you did not study for an upcoming test? Or maybe you so wanted to believe that there would be no consequences to eating a food to which you are allergic that you disregarded what you knew to be true. Because many of the

Come, My Beloved

One of the Safed kabbalists, the poet Solomon Halevy Alkabetz, composed the poem *"Lecha Dodi"* ("Come, My Beloved"), which Jews throughout the world sing on Friday evening as they greet Shabbat. Its next-to-last stanza reveals the poet's deepest hopes:

> Right and left, burst forward,
> And honor Adonai.
> One from Peretz's line [the Messiah] is coming,
> And we will rejoice and find delight.

The Shulhan Aruch Helps Unify the Jews

Rabbi Joseph Caro further strengthened the power of Jews to repair the world by observing *mitzvot*. Having fled from Spain, to Portugal, to the Balkan states, and finally to Safed, he witnessed firsthand the many disagreements among Jews as to how laws and customs should be observed. To solve this problem and promote Jewish unity, Caro published the *Shulhan Aruch,* meaning the "Prepared Table," in 1565. This book clearly described how Jewish law should be practiced.

Thanks to the newly invented printing press, the *Shulhan Aruch* was widely circulated. It became the best place for individual Jews to find answers to their religious questions. While different customs and traditions persisted, particularly between Sephardic and Ashkenazic Jews, the *Shulhan Aruch* remains to this day the code of Jewish law that traditional Jews turn to first when they have a religious question.

refugees of the Sephardic Diaspora yearned for the coming of the Messiah, they were willing to believe in men who were not worthy spiritual leaders. Several such men attracted large followings by claiming to be the Messiah.

One of the most infamous of the false messiahs was Shabbetai Zevi, a Jew from Turkey. Shabbetai Zevi spent his youth studying Kabbalah. He traveled to Israel and gained followers, including a brilliant student from Gaza named Nathan. In 1665 Nathan announced that he was the prophet Elijah and that Shabbetai Zevi was the long-awaited "King Messiah." Nathan declared that the world was finally "repaired" and would soon be redeemed, or returned to a more perfect state.

Shabbetai Zevi quickly built a huge following among both Sephardic and Ashkenazic Jews throughout the Ottoman Empire and Europe. Meanwhile, Jews who had doubts about Shabbetai Zevi quietly waited to see what would happen.

The Development of Jewish Law

The Torah is at the center of Jewish law. Over the centuries, the law has evolved based on the rulings, commentaries, and compilations of our sages and rabbis. This chart shows the main progression through the sixteenth century.

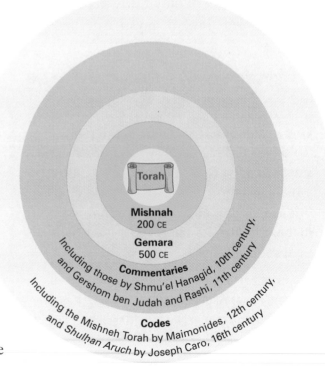

Torah

Mishnah
200 CE

Gemara
500 CE

Commentaries
Including those by Shmu'el Hanagid, 10th century, and Gershom ben Judah and Rashi, 11th century

Codes
Including the Mishneh Torah by Maimonides, 12th century, and Shulhan Aruch by Joseph Caro, 16th century

Shabbetai Zevi's followers believed he was born on the ninth of Av (Tisha B'Av), in keeping with the tradition that the Messiah would be born on the anniversary of the Temple's destruction. He died in 1676 on Yom Kippur.

Alarmed by the growing messianic movement, the Ottoman government arrested Shabbetai Zevi in 1666. They gave him a choice: convert to Islam or die. He converted. Deeply shaken, most of his supporters quickly abandoned Shabbetai Zevi. But some sought to justify his conversion and continued to believe in him. Not even his death, in 1676, convinced them that he was a false messiah.

Say What You Think

In the Dutch city of Amsterdam, meanwhile, some Sephardic Jews were working on entirely different ideas about how to repair the world. Inspired by freedom they had never known in Spain or Portugal, Jews explored both religious and secular subjects, such as science and philosophy. Freedom of thought and expression, they came to believe, was the key to improving the world.

One of the leading thinkers was Baruch (Benedict) Spinoza, born in 1632 in Amsterdam to a family of former secret-Jews. From a young age, Spinoza was unusually well read and had a strong curiosity. He studied with the city's leading rabbis, learned Latin, read the latest philosophical works, and spoke with the brightest and best educated people of his day. The more he studied, the more he questioned basic Jewish beliefs. Was Adam really the first human being? Did Moses really write down the Torah?

Such questions threatened the belief system of the mainstream Jewish community. It might have endangered Holland's small Jewish community, which worried that it would be blamed for permitting one of its members to spread "heretical" ideas. And so, in 1656, Amsterdam's rabbis excommunicated Spinoza, officially cutting him off "from the nation of Israel." Rather than repent, Spinoza insisted on his right to think and write freely. His writings, which have influenced both modern philosophy and modern biblical scholarship, stress the importance of human reason and freedom of thought. "Every man," Spinoza wrote, "should think what he wants and say what he thinks."

Keep in Touch!

Regardless of *where* they settled—in the Old World or in the New—and regardless of *how* they practiced Judaism—in secret or in public—Jews in the Sephardic Diaspora

This Dutch postage stamp, issued in 1977, honored Spinoza on the three hundredth anniversary of his death.

What Do You Think?

Although Spinoza was excommunicated, he never converted to another religion. If he were alive today, do you think that Spinoza would be accepted by the North American and Dutch Jewish communities? Why or why not?

Why might it be easier for today's Jewish communities to accept differences among their members? Why might it sometimes still be difficult?

remained connected to one another. They were united by their common origins in Spain and Portugal, their shared religious and social traditions, and their close family ties. Generations of Sephardic Jews helped, married, and traded with one another, reinforcing their friendships and family connections.

Judaism was by now long divided into two distinctive branches. One branch consisted of Sephardic Jews with roots in Spain and Portugal, and the other consisted of Ashkenazic Jews with roots in Germany and France. Many Jewish communities had two synagogues, one for Sephardic Jews and another for Ashkenazic Jews. In some communities Sephardic and Ashkenazic Jews rarely interacted and would not even marry one another.

But the experience of the Sephardic Jews left its mark on *all* Jews.

First, Jews learned never to take their security for granted. Even in a country where they had flourished for centuries, conditions could change for the worse and Jews could be persecuted and forced to leave. Second, the Inquisition reminded Jews to value the ties that united all Jewish people, no matter what their differences. By risking their lives to help one another, they succeeded in holding on to their religious beliefs and identities for generations, if only in secret. Finally, both Sephardic and Ashkenazic Jews were reminded that they had to be flexible and adaptable, and never give up hope. Working together, they could survive, strengthen Jewish life, and help to repair the world.

then & NOW

Rabbi Isaac Luria encouraged his followers to help repair the world through prayer, meditation, and observing *mitzvot*. In the twentieth century, Jewish thinkers broadened the concept of *tikun* to *tikun olam,* or acts of social justice that make the world a better place.

1. Why might the concept of *tikun* have comforted Jews who were anxious for the Messiah to arrive, bringing with him an end to suffering?

   _____

   _____

2. How can acts of *tikun olam* help inspire people today to believe that the world can become a better place?

   _____

   _____

3. Describe an act of *tikun olam* that you can perform. How can it help make the world a better place?

   _____

   _____

Chapter 10

The Polish Kehillah and German Enlightenment

Models of Isolation and Integration

investigate

- What caused Jewish life to become more diversified?

- Why did Jews become more involved with the larger secular community?

- How might the experience of the seventeenth- and eighteenth-century Jews of Poland and Lithuania have influenced our modern Jewish communities?

Key Words and Places

Kehillah	Ḥasidism
Shtetls	*Mitnagdim*
Council of the Four Lands	Enlightenment (*Haskalah*)
Techines	*Maskilim*
The Deluge	

The BIG Picture

Our story has been moving back and forth between Sepharad and Ashkenaz. Now we pick up the trail of the Ashkenazic Jews who were driven out of Western Europe and settled in Poland and Lithuania. Beginning in the 1500's, these Eastern European lands became leading centers of Jewish life where Jews experienced increasing opportunities for self-rule.

The Jews of Eastern Europe were largely separated from non-Jews. Christians and Jews lived on different streets, spoke different languages among themselves, wore different clothing, observed different holidays, attended different schools, worshipped in different ways, and even had different tax and court systems. But the Jews were not completely isolated. Exciting and challenging new ideas reached their towns from the larger secular community, as did episodes of sudden, anti-Jewish violence.

1500's	1516	mid-1500's	1564	1648
Eastern European lands become leading centers of Jewish life	First Jewish ghetto founded in Venice, Italy	Polish Jews establish the Council of the Four Lands	**World History:** William Shakespeare born in England	Bogdan Chmielnicki leads revolts against Polish nobles

Living Apart

Community has always been at the center of Jewish life. To this day, Jewish communal organizations, such as synagogues and religious schools, attend to the essential needs of Jewish life. They provide places for worship, educational services, social and political networks, and tzedakah for those in need. Jewish life in Poland and Lithuania also revolved around the *kehillah,* or organized Jewish community.

In America, where religion and government are separated by law, it is a matter of personal choice to participate in the Jewish community. In contrast, in Eastern Europe, where religion and government were closely linked, every Jew was legally *required* by the secular government to belong to the organized Jewish community. It legally represented the Jewish community to the government, it passed laws that all Jews had to follow, and it levied taxes that all Jews had to pay.

The requirement that Jews be members of the *kehillah* led to the strict segregation of Jews from non-Jews. But Jewish leaders took pride in their community's distinct lifestyle. They believed that segregation strengthened Jewish life, promoted the observance of Jewish law, and prevented intermarriage and assimilation. But it also prevented Jews and their neighbors from learning about and from one another, and it sowed the seeds of misunderstanding and mistrust.

about 1700

Baal Shem Tov, founder of Hasidism, born

1720

Elijah ben Solomon Zalman (Vilna Gaon) born; becomes great scholar

1770's

Enlightenment movement becomes known among Jews as *Haskalah*

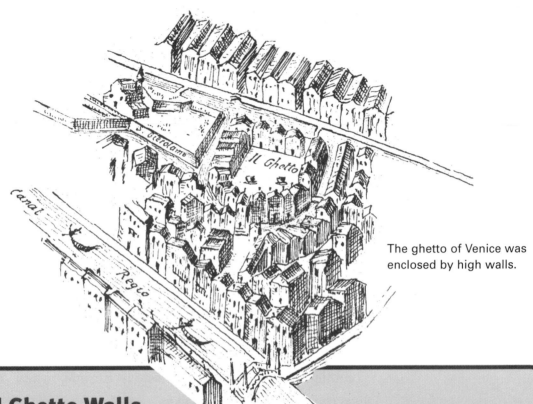

The ghetto of Venice was enclosed by high walls.

Behind Ghetto Walls

You have probably heard the word *ghetto* used today to describe poor urban neighborhoods. But *ghetto* originally referred specifically to Jewish neighborhoods. In 1509, a small group of Jews moved from Germany to the Italian city of Venice. They were eventually allowed to stay—but only if they lived in a very limited area enclosed by a high wall. Established in 1516, this Jewish neighborhood was called Ghetto. It was named for the nearby *ghetto,* or foundry—a place where metal is melted and molded.

The policy of requiring Jews to live in ghettos spread to other cities in Italy and parts of Central Europe. Ghetto gates were usually locked at night, to keep Jews inside and to protect them from non-Jews who remained outside. These walled neighborhoods became extremely crowded as Jewish populations grew. Still, Jews managed to thrive by working, studying, and worshipping together and by helping one another through hard times.

In what ways are modern ghettos similar to those that were first established for Jews? In what ways are they different?

Similar _____

_____

Different _____

_____

Yiddish was the main language of the Jews of Eastern Europe. A mixture of Hebrew, Aramaic, and German, it had first developed in Germany. In the countryside, the Jews built their communities in **shtetls**—Yiddish for "little towns." Shtetls were made up of a few streets of small wooden homes, shops, and a synagogue, which was at the center of shtetl life. In larger cities, Jews tended to live in "Jewish quarters," neighborhoods that were largely separated from non-Jews.

Determined to be self-governing in a land in which Catholicism was the state-sponsored religion, leading Jews from both cities and small towns in Poland formed a central Jewish government called the **Council of the Four Lands**. (The "Four Lands" refer to Poland's major provinces.) The council maintained its authority from the middle of the sixteenth century to the middle of the eighteenth century.

The Wolpa Synagogue in Wolpa, Poland, was built in 1643. According to an old story, a Polish prince was passing through Wolpa when his son became very ill. The Jewish community prayed for and took care of the boy. It is said that when his son recovered, the prince expressed his gratitude by giving the congregation money to build the synagogue.

From Prosperity to Catastrophe

From about the middle of the sixteenth century to the late nineteenth century, the Jews thrived in Poland. They worked as merchants, traders, and craftspeople. They also managed the estates of Polish nobles, supervised farms, and harvested timber. Some lived in large houses and amassed huge fortunes.

Thanks largely to this prosperity, Poland became a great center of Jewish learning, with a focus on the study of the Talmud and its commentaries. Academies sprang up in many cities. It was said that in the vast majority of Jewish homes in the kingdom of Poland, at least

This is a rare example of an illustrated sixteenth- or seventeenth-century prayer book from Poland. It is open to a page with a prayer for the welfare of the synagogue and community.

Jewish Self-Government

Just as the exilarchs of ancient Babylonia and the *parnasim* of medieval Sepharad and Ashkenaz oversaw Jewish communal concerns, so, too, did the Council of Four Lands. The council issued laws, collected taxes, and settled disputes among Jewish communities. Council members usually met twice a year, gathering at important trading fairs.

This was not exactly the form of democracy we enjoy today—power was in the hands of just a few wealthy council leaders. But the council was a source of pride for Polish Jews. Thanks to it, the Jews largely governed themselves, under the protection of the Polish king.

Why do you think the Jews preferred to be self-governing?

_____

_____

_____

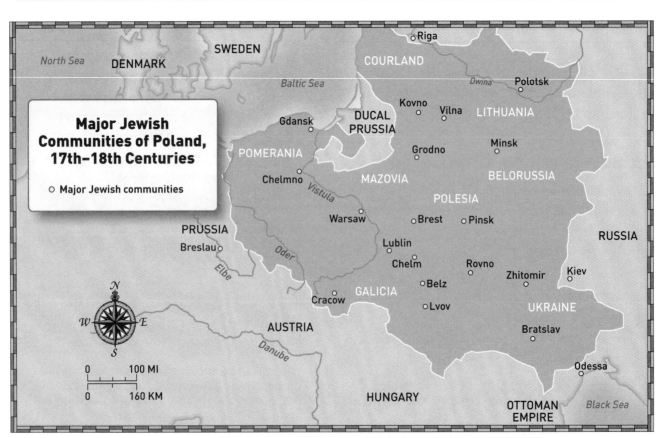

Large numbers of German Jews moved to Poland from the fourteenth through the sixteenth centuries. There they found a more welcoming environment and greater economic opportunities.

Glückel of Hamelin

Glückel of Hamelin lived in seventeenth-century Germany. As was the custom, by age thirteen Glückel was married. She worked with her husband in the seed pearl trade. Together, they built a successful business and had thirteen children.

Glückel wrote a detailed diary, which was published after her death. It tells much about the daily life of European Jews in the seventeenth century. Glückel wrote about her childhood, her marriage, her children, and her in-laws' plans to follow the Turkish Jew Shabbetai Zevi to Palestine, believing that he was the Messiah.

Glückel also wrote about her business: "I had an excellent business in seed pearls. I purchased [seed pearls] from all the Jews, picked and sorted the pearls, then sold them where I knew they were wanted."

Jews Move Back to Western Europe

In the 1600's, Jews began moving back to Western Europe. The Inquisition in Portugal and the massacres in Ukraine encouraged the Sephardic crypto-Jews and Ashkenazic Jews to make new homes in France, Italy, and Holland. In 1656, Jews also began to move back to England, although no law—since their expulsion in 1290—had been passed to officially permit them to return.

one member of the family was engaged in serious Judaic study.

Focused on Jewish life and law, the Jews unfortunately failed to notice the suffering of those around them. Polish peasants, as well as the neighboring Ukrainians, were brutally oppressed by Polish nobles. In 1648, these oppressed peoples revolted under the leadership of Bogdan Chmielnicki.

In a period known in Poland as **The Deluge,** bloody battles raged between Chmielnicki's supporters and the Polish nobles. The Jews were caught in the middle of this war. For years, some had worked for Polish nobles, managing their estates and collecting taxes. Chmielnicki associated all Jews with the hated nobles and their policies. As many as one out of every four Polish Jews died during The Deluge. Many of them were brutally massacred by Chmielnicki and his followers.

Jews with Different Views

In the aftermath of The Deluge, some Jews began to move westward into Germany and the countries of Western Europe. But most Polish Jews stayed and attempted to rebuild. This was especially true in Lithuania. Vilna, the capital of Lithuania, became a new center of Jewish life and learning. Its reputation grew so great that it became known as the "Jerusalem of Lithuania."

The leading scholar of Vilna was Elijah ben Solomon Zalman, known as the Vilna Gaon, the genius of Vilna. He lived from 1720 to 1797—about the time that George Washington lived. No branch of Jewish learning went unexplored by the Vilna Gaon. In addition to Torah, Talmud, and Jewish mysticism, he also studied Hebrew works on astronomy, geometry, algebra, geography, grammar, and medicine. He believed that all these subjects were necessary to fully understand Jewish law. The focus of Judaism, as he taught it, was in study. To him, study was even more important than prayer.

A growing movement known as **Hasidism** did not share the Vilna Gaon's priorities. The Hebrew word *hasid* means "pious," and to followers of the Hasidic movement, simple piety—the joy of worshipping God with all one's might—was more important than study.

The founder of Hasidism is believed to have been Israel ben Eliezer, also known as the Ba'al Shem Tov, meaning "Master of the Divine Name." The Ba'al Shem Tov was born around 1700 and died in 1760. He taught that even those who lacked education could still embrace God by praying, singing, and dancing with joyful passion and by observing *mitzvot*. "What is important," he declared, "is not how many

Hasidic Tales

The ancient sages taught many lessons by creating *midrashim,* or stories based on biblical texts. So, too, did the great Hasidic rabbis teach through stories.

The story is told of the Hasidic rabbi Moses of Kobryn who, upon looking up at the sky, cried: "Dear Angel! It is no trick to be an angel in heaven. You don't have to eat and drink and earn money. Come down to earth and worry about these things, and we shall see if you remain an angel" (Martin Buber, *Tales of Hasidism*).

Why might this story have comforted the followers of Hasidism?

_____

_____

How would you describe to a visiting angel the challenges of being a boy or girl your age?

_____

_____

_____

_____

Today, Hasidic men usually wear long, black, belted robes. Married men often wear fur hats on Shabbat and other festive occasions. The style of their dress is quite similar to that worn by Eastern European noblemen over two hundred years ago.

commandments we obey, but rather the spirit with which we obey them."

The Ba'al Shem Tov was twenty years older than the Vilna Gaon and came from modest roots. His teachings were often delivered through stories that uplifted and strengthened the spirits of humble Jews. Many such Jews had suffered at the hands of Chmielnicki. Also, they had felt powerless in the face of the wealthy Jewish community leaders. Now, through the Ba'al Shem Tov, they gained a sense of power.

As the Ba'al Shem Tov's followers widely spread his ideas throughout Eastern Europe, the Vilna Gaon and his followers sought to stamp out the Ḥasidic movement. Calling

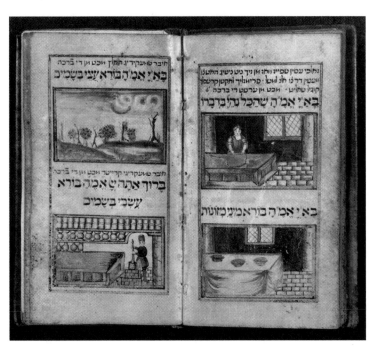

This eighteenth-century book from Tzelem, Hungary contains Hebrew blessings and prayers that were recited by women. In small communities, it was the custom for a father-in-law to give his new daughter-in-law such a book. He would then teach her when to say each prayer and blessing.

Techines: Personal Prayers

An adaptation that enabled larger numbers of Jews, particularly women, to participate more fully in Judaism was the translation of personal prayers from Hebrew into Yiddish. In addition, new prayers were written in Yiddish for women. These prayers were called *techines* (singular: *techine*).

Many *techines* were written by women as prayers for the welfare of children and husbands. *Techines* generally were addressed to "God of our Mothers, Sarah, Rebecca, Rachel, and Leah." For example, a *techine* written by Serel Rapoport pleads with our matriarch Sarah: "Mother, have mercy on us, your children, and pray for our children, that they not be separated from us."

Today, following in the tradition of *techines,* some synagogues encourage congregants to write personal prayers in English for life-cycle events, such as baby namings and bar and bat mitzvah services.

Write a personal prayer for the well-being of your family or a friend.

_____

_____

_____

_____

themselves *Mitnagdim* (opponents), they attacked Ḥasidim, warning that passionate singing and dancing were no substitute for devotion to the study of Torah. They thought that Jews should focus on Jewish learning and the strict fulfillment of each commandment.

Over the years, the Ḥasidim and *Mitnagdim* influenced one another, but their priorities remained different. The two groups followed different rabbis, used different prayer books, and observed different customs. In the end, however, they both contributed to Judaism by developing unique ideas of what it means to be a Jew and creating new options in Jewish life—options that enrich Judaism to this day.

"Dare to Know!"

In the early 1700's, modern ideas about freedom of thought and about truth were spreading to Jewish communities in western Poland and Germany. Many were similar to the statement of the Jewish-Dutch philosopher Baruch Spinoza that "every man should think what he wants and say what he thinks."

Supporters of these new ideas insisted that truth could be discovered by individuals through scientific experimentation and reason. Above all, they placed their faith in the creative powers of the human mind. By the 1770's, this movement, which many call the **Enlightenment,** became known among Jews as the *Haskalah.* (*Haskalah* is the Hebrew word for "enlightenment.") Jews who followed this path were known as *Maskilim,* meaning "enlightened ones."

The ideals of the Enlightenment have helped create open and tolerant societies in North America. It is easier than ever to maintain one's Jewish identity and succeed in the secular world. On Rosh Hashanah, the tolerance and acceptance of our non-Jewish neighbors can be seen as we are wished a happy New Year on storefronts, Web sites, radio, and television.

Instead of focusing on Jewish law, like the *Mitnagdim,* or on piety, like the Ḥasidim, followers of the *Haskalah* sought to open Jewish life to the latest scientific and philosophical ideas from the non-Jewish world. They believed that Jews should become broadly educated and seek truth everywhere. In response, increasing numbers of Jews began to attend universities. The German Enlightenment philosopher Immanuel Kant had a particularly

Moses Mendelssohn

Among the small group of Jews who developed Enlightenment ideas, the best known was Moses Mendelssohn. Mendelssohn lived from 1729 to 1786, the same period as the Vilna Gaon, the Ba'al Shem Tov, and Thomas Jefferson. The child of a poor Hebrew scribe, he was small and bent over, suffering from a deformed spine. But Mendelssohn proved to be a brilliant student and at age fourteen he set out for Berlin from his hometown of Dessau. In Berlin he studied not only the Bible and the Talmud, but also Jewish philosophy, general philosophy, Hebrew, Latin, Greek, modern languages, and mathematics.

Traditional rabbis worried that people who followed Mendelssohn's path would give in to the social pressure to convert. This is just what happened when some of Mendelssohn's own children converted to Christianity. How might the ideals of freedom and tolerance have made it easier for them to abandon Judaism?

Mendelssohn remained a faithful Jew even as he befriended and shared ideas with non-Jews. He called upon Jews and non-Jews to pursue truth and to support the ideals of freedom and tolerance. As long as someone is honest and law-abiding, he wrote, that person should "be allowed to speak as he thinks, to speak to God in his own way...and to seek eternal salvation wherever he thinks he can find it."

Do you think Mendelssohn's ideas would have been of interest to Thomas Jefferson and other Americans of his time? Why or why not?

_____

_____

_____

Three Adaptations to Life in Poland and Lithuania

ḤASIDIM	MITNAGDIM	MASKILIM
You don't need to be highly educated. Pray and perform *mitzvot* with passion and joy.	Study Jewish law and strictly observe *mitzvot*.	Study science, reason, philosophy, and Judaism; then make personal decisions about what to believe and how to live.

great influence on the *Maskilim*. "Dare to know!" he had proclaimed. "Have the courage and strength to use your own intellect."

Change Is in the Air

For many, the *Haskalah* challenged the authority of traditional rabbis and challenged the basis of Jewish separatism. Most important, it created a new type of Jewish leader—the *Maskil*. The *Maskil* was not a rabbi or a traditional student of religious texts, but instead a thinker, a writer, and a scholar, at home with both Jewish and secular culture.

The *Haskalah* paved the way for Jews to become integrated into modern society. By teaching Jews about the world around them, it helped change their attitudes toward non-Jews and, in time, non-Jewish attitudes toward them. It created the ideal of the Jew who masters both secular and Jewish learning, and it made it possible for Jews to live and work with non-Jewish neighbors. It prepared our people for

many of the opportunities *and* challenges of modern Jewish life.

To this day, there are times when we still feel conflicted about our commitments as Jews and our participation in secular life. Such conflicts may arise when a test is scheduled at public school on Yom Kippur or when nonkosher food is served at a public gathering. But we also value the freedom to solve such problems.

At times, we still find ourselves torn between the Ḥasidim's focus on the joy of being Jewish, the *Mitnagdim's* focus on Jewish learning and law, and the *Maskilim's* focus on reason and cultural enlightenment. But all three movements have enriched modern Judaism by showing us diverse ways to live meaningful Jewish lives.

Today we take for granted the right to live freely as both Jews and full citizens of our country. We expect to enjoy the same rights and opportunities as all other citizens. The Jews of Europe, even at the time of the Enlightenment, did not enjoy this freedom. Fortunately, that was about to change.

then & NOW

In every period of Jewish history there has been more than one way to live as a Jew. In ancient Israel one might have been a Pharisee, Sadducee, Essene, or Zealot. In the eighteenth-century East European Diaspora one might have been a Ḥasid, *Mitnaged,* or *Maskil*. And today, in North America, one might be a Reform, Conservative, Reconstructionist, Orthodox, ultra-Orthodox, secular, or other type of Jew.

1. Interview three Jewish people—classmates, family members, friends, or neighbors. Describe two ways in which their beliefs or Jewish practices are similar and two ways in which they are different. You may want to brainstorm with your classmates about questions to ask before conducting your interviews.

Similarities	Differences
A. _____	A. _____
_____	_____
B. _____	B. _____
_____	_____

2. How might their similarities help unite the Jewish community?

_____

_____

3. How might their differences help enrich the Jewish community?

_____

_____

Chapter 11 Revolution and Emancipation

The Challenge of Freedom

investigate

- What opportunities did emancipation bring to the average Jew?

- What challenges came with increased freedom?

- How do those same challenges affect us today?

Key Words and Places

Continental Congress	U.S. Constitution
American Revolution	Separation of Church and State
Declaration of Independence	French Revolution

The BIG Picture

What comes to mind when you hear the word *emancipation*? As a twenty-first-century American, you might think of the end of slavery in the United States, or the Nineteenth Amendment to the U.S. Constitution, which gave women the right to vote. But had you been a nineteenth-century European Jew, you probably would think of your own struggle for equal rights.

Most Jews lived in countries that denied them the full rights of citizens, such as the right to vote, run for public office, or own land. Emancipation meant the ending of these restrictions; it meant that Jews could eventually become full-fledged citizens.

Before emancipation, Jews were often forced to live separately. They also were often pressured by their community—family, friends, neighbors—to follow Jewish law and tradition. After emancipation, they no longer had to actively maintain their Jewish identities or their ties to the Jewish community. Both decisions became matters of personal choice. They remain matters of personal choice today in democratic countries, and this fact continues to shape Judaism.

1654
First North American Jewish community founded

1776
Continental Congress declares independence of United States

1787
United States Constitution written

1789
French Revolution begins

Freedom's Call

As Protestant countries established colonies in the New World, Diaspora Jews made the great journey and settled in them. Colonies such as Recife in Brazil, Curacao, Jamaica, Surinam in the West Indies, and New Amsterdam (later called New York) became home to significant Sephardic Jewish communities.

The first Jewish community in North America was founded in 1654 by twenty-three Sephardic Jews who settled in New Amsterdam. Over the next century, the Jewish population of Britain's thirteen American colonies grew to about twenty-five hundred. These colonial Jews lived mainly in the East Coast port cities of Savannah, Charleston, Philadelphia, New York, and Newport. Many were shopkeepers who sold hardware and dry goods such as fabric and needles; others were merchants, farmers, silversmiths, tailors, bakers, tobacconists, and saddlers. While these Jews did not have equal rights with Christians, they were safer and enjoyed more freedom than Jews in other parts of the world.

1791
French Jews granted full citizenship and legal equality

1818
World History: *Frankenstein,* by English author Mary Shelly, is published

1858
Jews gain right to hold seats in British Parliament

1871
German Jews given complete legal emancipation

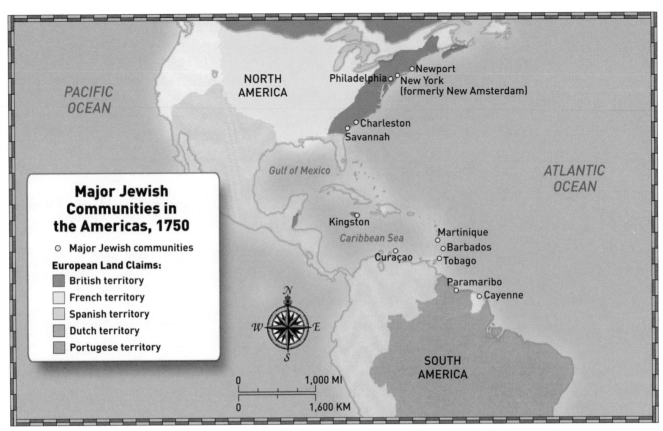

Although there were Ashkenazic Jews in North America in 1750, the synagogues were Sephardic. These communities shared close cultural and business ties with other Sephardic communities on the Atlantic seaboard, including those in the Caribbean, South America, and Western Europe. For example, if a synagogue in New York needed a Torah scroll, it might write to a synagogue in the Caribbean for assistance.

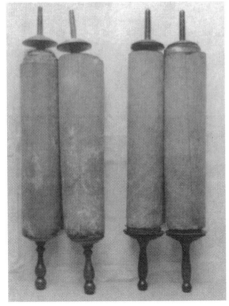

These Torah scrolls were brought to Savannah, Georgia, in 1733 and 1737.

By the early 1770's, the Jews were as angered by British taxes and policies as were the other colonists. And when the **Continental Congress** declared independence in 1776, most Jews sided with the new nation. As many as one hundred Jews fought against the British in the **American Revolution**.

The peace treaty ending the Revolutionary War and recognizing the independence of the American colonies was signed in 1783. The Jews eagerly watched to see what their legal status would be in this new nation. Would colonial-era restrictions on their ability to vote and run for office be lifted? Would the

This famous painting by Emanuel Leutz shows George Washington and his soldiers crossing the Delaware River.

statement in the **Declaration of Independence** that all people "are created equal" apply to them?

The answer came in the form of the **U.S. Constitution** written in 1787. The Constitution made religious liberty a basic right. Religious tests that had been used to qualify people for political office were outlawed. And, most famously, the federal Constitution's First Amendment (1791) declared that "Congress shall make no law respecting an establishment of religion, or prohibiting the free exercise thereof." This idea is often referred to as the **separation of church and state**.

Haym Salomon

The best-known Jewish patriot of the revolutionary era, Haym Salomon, was born in Poland around 1740. Settling in New York City in 1772, Salomon became a successful merchant and a supporter of American independence. He was arrested for anti-British activities when the British occupied New York City.

Salomon was freed when the British learned that he spoke fluent German. They made him an interpreter for the German mercenaries, soldiers from Germany hired to fight in the British army. Salomon used this opportunity to persuade the mercenaries to desert to the American side. For this, the British charged him with being a spy (which he was) and sentenced him to hang. But he escaped and made his way to Philadelphia. There he raised money for the revolutionary government and the Continental army.

Salomon was deeply committed to the ideals of freedom. What cause is important to you? Why? What actions are you willing to take to support it?

_____

_____

_____

A Symbol of Freedom

Throughout history, the biblical story of the Israelites' Exodus from Egypt has been an inspiration for the liberation of oppressed peoples. One design proposed in 1782 for the official seal of the United States illustrated the splitting of the Sea of Reeds and the escape of the Israelites.

Explain the meaning of "Rebellion to tyrants is obedience to God."

_____

_____

Do you agree or disagree with the statement? Why?

_____

_____

This U.S. postage stamp honors Hanukkah. Do you think such stamps violate the separation of church and state because they are produced by the federal government and honor religious holidays? Why or why not?

STATE-SPONSORED RELIGION	SEPARATION OF CHURCH AND STATE
The government recognizes one or more religions as state religions.	The government has no official religion.
Religions that are not recognized by the state have restrictions imposed on them.	All religions are equal in the eyes of the government.
State taxes support religious institutions, such as churches and synagogues.	No state funds support religious institutions; instead, religious institutions depend on voluntary contributions.

History in the Making: Religious Freedom

Despite the new government's guarantee of religious freedom, at first not every state in the Union honored that guarantee. In practice, some gave only Protestants full rights. Although it took one hundred years, by the end of the eighteenth century most American Jewish men enjoyed both the right to vote and the right to be elected to governmental office.

The United States now treated Jews as independent, individual citizens, with the same legal rights as all other citizens. Importantly, they received these rights under the U.S. Constitution along with other Americans, not, as in so many European countries, through a separate privilege or, as it was often called, a "Jew bill" that set Jews apart as a group.

Imagine that you are a Jew living in America in 1791. As Rosh Hashanah approaches, you write to your relatives in Poland. In the space below, compare and contrast your life as a Jew in America with your life in Poland.

Dear Family, _____

_____

_____

_____

_____

_____

_____

_____

_____

_____

On August 17, 1790, George Washington visited Newport, Rhode Island. While there, Moses Seixas of Congregation Jeshuat Israel presented him with a letter expressing the Jewish community's loyalty to the new nation. Washington responded in his own letter, shown here. He wrote "May the Children of the Stock of Abraham, who dwell in this land, continue to merit and enjoy the good will of the other Inhabitants…"

France Breaks with the Past

The success and ideals of the American Revolution inspired change in Europe, beginning with the **French Revolution** in 1789. That nation's eight-hundred-year-old monarchy was suddenly swept from power. "All men are born and remain free, and are equal in rights," declared the new revolutionary National Assembly in France. "No one will be mistreated for his opinions, even for religious opinions."

Despite these changes in France, Jews could neither be citizens nor run for public office. Instead, they remained organized into traditional self-governing communities, living in four areas on the country's outer edges. But if the French Declaration of Rights did not immediately affect France's forty thousand Jews, it did offer them hope.

Inspired by the United States' Declaration of Independence and the Revolutionary War, equality soon sparked a wondrous change in Jewish life. In 1791, after much debate, Jews were granted full citizenship and legal equality with other French men and women. Discriminatory taxes and degrading anti-Jewish laws were abolished.

Freedom Brings New Challenges

In the years following the French Revolution, Jews enjoyed the status of full-fledged French citizenship. But freedom brought new challenges. French Jews had always lived in separate, self-governing religious communities, just as the Jews of Babylonia, Spain, and Poland had. In contrast to their non-Jewish neighbors, Jews lived according to the rhythms of the Jewish calendar and under the guidelines set forth by Jewish law.

That quickly changed. French leaders expected Jews to adapt to the larger French culture. "To the Jews as a nation, nothing; to the Jews as individuals, everything," one French supporter of equality for Jews declared. In other words, Jews had to accept the authority of secular judges and courts in place of their own, separate legal system. By focusing on individual Jews rather than on Jews as a group, French supporters of equality believed that eventually Jews would become like all other French citizens. They would lose their distinguishing Jewish characteristics.

Emancipation Spreads

Napoleon used his powerful military to spread the French Revolution by force, marching his troops into Belgium, the Netherlands, southern Germany, and Italy. In the lands he conquered, Napoleon sought to extend the principles of the revolution. This included the emancipation of the Jews. Working side by side, French soldiers and young Jews tore down the ghetto walls that had isolated European Jewish communities for centuries. Jews were freed and granted legal equality on the same basis as the Jews in France.

But in some places, when the French armies retreated, the old anti-Jewish laws were revived. Particularly in Frankfurt, as well as in other places including Bavaria and Baden, promises were made on paper to Jews but never delivered. Some European rabbis welcomed laws that restricted Jews. They feared that Jews would shed their Jewish values and ties if they were free to live as equals among non-Jews.

But the majority of European Jews craved the rights and privileges of citizenship. They saw that emancipated Jews enjoyed many more options of where to live and work. Emancipated Jews dressed as they pleased, educated their children in the best schools, and participated in public life. Emancipation, they insisted, did not mean the end of Judaism—instead it offered new and exciting ways to live as Jews.

A Double-Edged Sword

The process of emancipation varied from country to country. Jews gained a great deal of freedom in England. But they won the right to

Napoleon's Questions

Jews were full citizens according to the law—but in practice suspicion and discrimination continued in France's everyday life. The emperor, Napoleon Bonaparte, was willing to promote the rights of Jews as full French citizens. But first he wanted Jewish leaders to prove that their religious beliefs did not conflict with the duties of French citizenship.

Imagine that you are a Jewish leader in France in the summer of 1806. As part of a group known as the Assembly of Jewish Notables, you have been asked by Napoleon to answer twelve questions concerning the relationship between Jewish law and French law. Here's one of them: "In the eyes of Jews, are French people considered as relatives or as strangers?" How might you respond? Why?

_____

_____

_____

The Jewish leaders' answers assured Napoleon that France's Jews were thoroughly patriotic.

hold seats in Parliament only in 1858, after a long political struggle. In some German states, Jews won and lost rights repeatedly as governments changed hands. Complete legal emancipation did not come to Germany until 1871. In Russia and Poland, where the majority of the world's Jews still lived, emancipation came only in the twentieth century, and was not fully enforced even then. As the Jews learned again and again, it takes more than legislation to stamp out prejudice.

In both Europe and the United States, emancipation proved to be a double-edged sword. On the one hand, it brought great benefits to Jews, such as expanded educational and economic possibilities and the opportunity to serve in government. On the other hand, emancipation carried the risk that Jews might decide to abandon their religious beliefs and practices. Now, not only could one choose to live as a Jew, one also could choose *not* to live as a Jew.

Grace Aguilar

Grace Aguilar (1816–1847) was an English Jew of Sephardic descent whose ancestors had been crypto-Jews. Aguilar believed that women should be taught to understand Jewish values and observances, not trained to blindly accept them. She also believed that new opportunities for Jewish education and spiritual growth were opening up in emancipated countries, like England and the United States. Aguilar insisted that Jews were now "free to become mentally and spiritually elevated."

In her book *The Spirit of Judaism,* Aguilar expressed not only her pride as a Jew but also her faith in an emancipated England. She wrote, "We shall go forth, no longer striving to conceal our religion through SHAME (for it can only be such a base emotion prompting us to conceal it in a free and happy England);—strengthened and sanctified by its blessed spirit, we shall feel the soul elevated within us."

Aguilar wrote several other books including *The Jewish Faith*. Written as a series of letters to a Jewish girl, the book offered spiritual and moral guidance. Aguilar also wrote *Women of Israel: Characters and Sketches from the Holy Scriptures,* which focused on the contributions of biblical women.

As a descendant of crypto-Jews, Jews who were persecuted and forced to practice Judaism in secret, why might Aguilar have felt so passionately about Jewish education?

_____

_____

_____

then & NOW

Before the French Revolution, French Jews were pressured to set themselves apart from non-Jews. After the emancipation, they were pressured to assimilate—to speak, dress, and act like those around them. Before they had seen themselves simply as Jews; now they identified as French men and women of the Jewish religion.

1. How does this remind you of your own experience as both a Jew and a citizen of this country?

_____

_____

_____

2. How is it different from your experience?

_____

_____

_____

3. Describe one valuable reason to actively maintain your Jewish identity in a free society.

_____

_____

_____

Chapter **12** Judaism and the Modern World

Finding a Balance

investigate

- How did changes in the modern world influence the Jews?
- What adaptations did Jews make to Judaism?
- What types of adaptations do we continue to make today?

Key Words and Places

Ḥeder	Orthodox Judaism
Reform Judaism	Czars
Conservative Judaism	Pale of Settlement

The **BIG** Picture

Throughout Jewish history our people have tried to strike a balance between Jewish tradition and modern ideas. Think back to the time when Judea was part of the Greek Empire. Many Jews selected elements of Greek culture—Greek language, names, styles of dress, and concepts of beauty—and integrated them into Jewish culture.

Jews have made such choices again and again—in ancient Babylonia, medieval Spain, eighteenth-century Poland, and nineteenth-century Europe. As Jews had done so many times before, newly emancipated European Jews struggled to find their place in a changing world. Some resisted modern culture. Others completely assimilated, shedding their Judaism in order to fit in. But, like most Jews who had lived before them, the vast majority chose the middle road. They refused to give up their heritage. Instead, they adapted Judaism to the changing times.

1784	**1831**	**by 1840's**	**mid-1800's**
Jewish philanthropist Moses Montefiore born in England	Zachariah Frankel becomes first rabbi in Bohemia with a secular education	Ideas of *Haskalah* begin to spread to Pale of Settlement (Poland)	Samuel Holdheim and Abraham Geiger help create what is now Reform Judaism

Jews Join the Middle Class

The years between 1815 and 1880 were ones of rapid change. The change was most obvious in Germany, home to the largest Jewish community in Western and Central Europe. In the early 1800's, the great majority of German-Jewish men were barely making a living in occupations that were considered dishonorable, such as peddling, money lending, and selling used clothes. At that same time, 20 percent of Jewish men were beggars or thieves. But by 1870, 80 percent of German Jewish wage earners had worked their way up to the middle and upper middle classes. Many were involved in trade and commerce, for example, as shopkeepers, merchants, and bankers.

If you had lived at this time, you would literally see—and *hear*—the changes taking place. Many Jews abandoned the distinctive style of dress that was common to Jews and they stopped speaking Yiddish. In their place, they adopted German fashions and language. Next, they abandoned the traditional Jewish school, the **ḥeder,** sending their children to secular schools or to schools that taught both secular and Jewish subjects. This broader education made it possible for many young Jews to pursue desirable jobs outside the Jewish community.

1855

Alexander II becomes czar of Russia; grants Jews more freedom

1876

World History: Alexander Graham Bell invents the telephone in the United States

1881

Czar Alexander II assassinated

A Jewish merchant selling used uniforms in about 1850

The Changing Family

Jewish families in nineteenth-century Europe were beginning to look and act more like their middle-class neighbors—and more like middle-class families in North America today. Men married later, waiting until they were financially secure. Couples had fewer children. Many Jews attended concerts and art exhibitions and sent their children to music lessons and gymnastics classes.

How is your family similar to the European Jewish family described above? How is it different?

Similar _____

_____

_____

Different _____

_____

_____

Soon many Jews accepted secular middle-class values. The time-honored ideal Jewish male, the Torah scholar, was replaced by a new ideal: the culturally well-rounded gentleman who knew the ways and values of the secular world. Women, who had traditionally helped their husbands in business, now focused on household duties. They became responsible for their children's religious development and education, duties to which Jewish men had attended. Some women extended their domestic obligations to include volunteer work for charity groups and educational organizations.

Two Different Experiences

Emancipation came at different times and in different ways throughout Europe. As a result, Jews had very different experiences as they entered the modern world. The cases of England and Germany highlight the differences.

In England, where emancipation was a slow process, the social and economic integration of Jews came early and with relative ease. Jews felt little pressure to abandon Jewish traditions. They took great pride in their synagogues, schools, and social welfare agencies. English Jews benefited from the tolerant attitude of

Moses Montefiore

British Jews were living well, but that did not lessen their sense of responsibility for Jews in other lands. One of the great Jewish philanthropists of this time was Moses Montefiore. He was born in 1784 to an Italian Jewish family that had settled in England. By the time he was forty, Montefiore had made a fortune as a stockbroker. He dedicated the next sixty-one years of his long life to helping Jews around the world.

Montefiore visited Palestine seven times. There he used his money to build homes, farms, and synagogues for the Jewish community. He traveled to Russia, Romania, Morocco, and other countries, urging world leaders to abolish anti-Jewish laws. In 1840, he learned that several Jews in Damascus, Syria, were accused of killing a Christian monk to use his blood in preparation for Passover. Shocked, Montefiore quickly organized a delegation to see the Syrian ruler and eventually won the Jews' release from prison.

Montefiore's actions helped create a model for communal support of Jews in other countries. Working with your teacher and classmates, search the Internet or contact your local Jewish Federation or other Jewish communal organization for information on how you can help Jewish communities in Israel and other countries. Record your findings here.

_____

_____

_____

_____

_____

Montefiore built this windmill in Jerusalem to provide a source of income for the settlement called Mishkenot She'ananim. Today, it houses a museum dedicated to the story of Montefiore's life.

Heinrich Heine referred to his baptism as a "ticket of admission to European culture." What do you think he meant?

secular educations and adopted the middle-class lifestyle of their neighbors while remaining faithful to their Judaism. Others gave up their Jewish beliefs and customs. Some went to the extreme of converting to Christianity.

The most famous convert was a brilliant young poet named Heinrich Heine, who lived from 1797 to 1856. Heine realized that, as a Jew, he could never advance in the academic world of Germany. So, when he was twenty-seven, he converted to Christianity. But Heine, and others who converted to advance their careers, found that even this most radical step did not satisfy their non-Jewish neighbors. After repeated attempts to secure a university position ended in failure, Heine left Germany for Paris. He later spoke regretfully about his conversion, telling a friend: "I make no secret of my Judaism, to which I have not returned, because I never left it."

Responding to Changing Times

German Jews tried to modernize themselves by adapting their Judaism to the changing times. In the process, they hoped the prejudice of their non-Jewish neighbors would disappear. They also hoped that a modernized Judaism would appeal to more Jews and encourage the many intellectuals who had abandoned Judaism to return. Their hopes inspired a variety of creative solutions.

Reform Judaism

Experimentation began in 1810, when Israel Jacobson, the head of the Jewish community in the German kingdom of Westphalia, dedicated a grand "temple" built to look like a church. It included an organ and a clock tower with a bell in it that pealed on the hour. Jacobson, often

many of their non-Jewish neighbors. For example, many Christians expected the Jews to remain a separate group and admired them for their ability to survive in the Diaspora.

The situation in Germany was quite different. Jewish emancipation had been imposed on the German states by Napoleon's conquering armies. After Napoleon's defeat, numerous states withdrew citizenship from their Jewish residents. Many Germans considered Jews unfit for citizenship. They believed that Judaism was backward and taught hatred of outsiders. Others worried that if the Jews integrated into society, they would compete for jobs with Christians. Jews found themselves barred from many professions and excluded from German society.

Frustrated, many Jews worked hard to prove they really could live both as Jews *and* as citizens of modern Germany. They pursued called "the Father of Reform," shortened the prayer service and made it more orderly and dignified. Soon, similar temples opened in Hamburg and Berlin.

More serious changes were introduced in 1819 when the Hamburg Temple adopted a prayer book that dropped all mention of a messiah. It also dropped all references to the Jews' return to the Land of Israel. Many Reformers were concerned that Jewish ties to Israel might cast doubt on German Jews' patriotism.

In the mid-1800's, two German rabbis, Samuel Holdheim and Abraham Geiger, helped create what we now call **Reform Judaism**. However, Reform leaders could not always agree on how quickly to push for change. Holdheim was willing to abandon all Jewish laws and traditions that separated Jews from non-Jews, including male circumcision and the ban on intermarriage. His Reform congregation in Berlin was the most radical in Germany. *Kippot* and *tallitot*, or prayer shawls, were not worn, and the shofar was no longer sounded on Rosh Hashanah.

Geiger believed that the Torah was written by human beings. He also insisted that throughout history, Judaism had adapted to the times and the needs of the Jews. However, Geiger did not support controversial innovations that threatened to divide the Jewish community. He believed that the value of Jewish unity, *klal Yisra'el*, required a more gradual approach to change, such as using German for some prayers and Hebrew for others.

In his sermons, Geiger emphasized what he called "prophetic Judaism." By this he meant the universal values taught by our ancient prophets, such as caring for the poor, the orphaned, and the widowed. Like the prophets, Geiger stressed the value of social justice.

Conservative Judaism

For many who supported the principle of change over time, the Reformers were moving too quickly and were too radical. The final straw came when some Reformers backed the elimination of Hebrew as the language of Jewish prayer.

Rabbi Zechariah Frankel, a moderate Reformer, argued that Hebrew should not be eliminated. He believed that it united world

Studying Torah and Jewish tradition helps us adapt to changing times while maintaining our core beliefs. Today, the Responsa Committee of the Central Conference of American Rabbis, an international organization of Reform rabbis, provides guidance on changes in Reform tradition. The committee members base their opinions on a scholarly review of both Jewish tradition and modern values. Individual Reform rabbis and congregations make decisions on how to apply the committee's recommendations in their communities.

Jewry and was a key to Jewish survival. Like other German Jews, Frankel and his supporters had no interest in reviving the Jewish nation as a political state in the Land of Israel. But they believed that Judaism was a culture as well as a religion. They did not want the cultural part of Judaism to be discarded.

Frankel's followers broke from the Reformers and became the forerunners of the Conservative movement. (**Conservative Judaism** did not formally become a movement until the twentieth century.) They retained Hebrew in their synagogue services along with prayers for the Messiah and the rebuilding of Zion (Jerusalem). Frankel advocated "positive historical Judaism," by which he meant that past Jewish experience was a positive value. While Frankel agreed with the Reformers that Judaism was an evolving tradition, he believed that changes should be made gradually, be based on historical research, and be respectful of Jewish law and the traditions of the people.

Orthodox Judaism

Not all Jews accepted the idea that Judaism needed modernization. Leading the struggle against the innovators was Moses Sofer, a respected rabbi in Hungary. Sofer rejected the idea of change. Even cultural adaptation must be opposed, he wrote, because it could lead to religious changes. "Be forewarned not to change your Jewish names, language, and clothing—God forbid…. Never say: 'Times have changed!' We have an old Father—praised be God's name—who has never changed and shall never change."

Other traditional Jews were eager to find ways of adapting to the modern world without abandoning Jewish law, or halachah. Led by Samson Raphael Hirsch, they became known as

Tradition and Change, Conservative Style

Like Reform Judaism, Conservative Judaism continues to adapt Judaism to meet the needs of the modern world. Where once there were no female Conservative rabbis, now there are many. And where once men and women sat separately during prayer services, and women were not permitted full religious rights and duties with men, now many Conservative congregations offer women full equality with men.

Conservative Judaism tries to innovate within the limits of halachah, or traditional Jewish law. The rabbis of the Committee on Jewish Law and Standards meet and rule on issues, such as whether or not it is permissible to drive to a synagogue on Shabbat.

If there is a clear majority, the ruling becomes a binding practice for the Conservative movement. If the vote is split, rabbis may choose to follow either the majority or minority opinion. Their individual choices are based on the needs and circumstances of their own congregations and on their own understanding of Jewish law.

"neo-Orthodox," meaning new Orthodox, to distinguish themselves from Sofer's "ultra-Orthodox" followers. (Neo-Orthodox Judaism was the forerunner of Modern **Orthodox Judaism**.)

Hirsch supported Jewish emancipation. He encouraged his followers to pursue a secular education and adopt the dress and language of

The Pale of Settlement

Area of the Pale of Settlement

○ Major Jewish community

By the end of the nineteenth century, there were almost five million Jews in the Pale of Settlement. The geographic locations on this map are labeled with their present-day names.

the larger society. He even allowed Jewish men to shave their beards. But Hirsch rejected the principle that halachah and Jewish rituals had changed over time. He believed that the Torah and its laws were revealed by God on Mount Sinai and could not be altered.

Little More Than a Dream

Emancipation was *delayed* until the mid-nineteenth century in Germany, but it was little more than a *dream* for the millions of Jews in the Russian Empire. In fact, the entire idea of a modern nation-state with citizens was foreign to the Russians. While Jews had no rights, neither did the rest of the population. Russian **czars** ruled without limits on their power.

Historically, Russia had been home to few Jews. But in the late 1700's, it conquered huge sections of Poland, which had a large Jewish population. Driven by anti-Jewish prejudice, Russian leaders decided they did not want the Jewish population to spread throughout Russia. They drew an imaginary line around part of the land that had once been Poland and declared that all Jews must live there. This area became known as the **Pale of Settlement.**

The czars hoped that the Jews would assimilate into Russian society and lose their connection to Judaism. One of the most effective government policies was the drafting of Jewish boys and men into the Russian army. During their long years of service, Jews could not observe their religion and were often pressured to convert to Christianity.

Parents would do almost anything to keep their sons out of the army. *Kehillah* leaders frequently arranged for the children of the rich and influential to avoid army service. They filled their community requirements by sending agents, called *chappers*, or snatchers, to kidnap children of the poor, who were then sent to the army. As a result, many Jews lost faith in their leaders and Jewish unity was severely weakened.

New Ideas Arrive

By the 1840's and 1850's, the ideas of the German-Jewish Enlightenment, or *Haskalah*, finally began to spread to the Pale. The Russian government actively encouraged Jewish modernization. In 1844, it opened new schools where Jewish children were taught the Russian language and culture. Traditional Jews were suspicious of the schools. But Russian Jews who favored modernization, known as *Maskilim*, supported them. They believed that a broad education was the key to social and economic advancement.

Russian Jewish supporters of Enlightenment ideas were given a new cause for optimism when Alexander II became the czar of Russia in 1855. Alexander II treated the Jews more humanely than previous rulers had. He even allowed some to leave the Pale. More Jews began studying at Russian high schools and universities. In time, a Jewish middle class developed in cities such as Warsaw, Cracow, Odessa, and St. Petersburg.

Everyday Life: Parents and Children

As Enlightenment spread to Russia in the 1840's, arguments between parents and children became a regular part of Jewish family life. "There was tremendous pressure for Enlightenment among young people," remembered Pauline Wengeroff (1833–1916), whose memoirs teach us much about Jewish life at the time. "No matter how angry and upset parents became, eventually they had to give in."

One day Pauline heard her older brothers-in-law talking excitedly about the arrival in town of modern books of science and literature. "We shall find the books," one of them said. "We will just have to be extremely careful and sneak the work into our Talmud time. But don't allow the parents to catch on."

Of course, the parents did catch on—Pauline's mother walked in on them and caught them studying German poetry. A bitter argument followed.

Whose side would you take in this argument? Why?

_____

_____

What advice would you give to help settle the dispute peaceably?

_____

_____

_____

In every family there are times when people agree with one another and times when they disagree. How can listening and speaking respectfully to others help avoid turning disagreements into arguments?

Awake My People

The spirit of the Enlightenment was captured by the Jewish poet Judah Leib Gordon in his 1866 poem, "Awake My People!"

Awake my people! How long will you sleep?

Night has passed and the sun is shining brightly...

This Land of Eden [Russia] now opens her gates to you,

Her sons now call you "brother"!

Unlike the Jews in western and central Europe, the Russian *maskilim* were not interested in reforming the Jewish religion. Those who wanted to maintain their Jewish identities created a secular Jewish culture. They devoted themselves to a revival of Yiddish and Hebrew culture, creating new literature and poetry in those languages.

Between Two Worlds

The rapid changes all over Europe left some Jews feeling as though they were living between two worlds, worlds that sometimes collided. A yeshiva student named Yeshaya Perelstein, who lived in a small Polish town in the mid-nineteenth century, became curious about the world around him. Although his father disapproved, he taught himself Russian and began to read the great books of Western literature. "A change came over me," he wrote. "I discovered…a universe that enchanted me with its originality, its beauty, its rich colors.… Slowly my heart was filled with doubt, doubt as to whether the Talmudic sages were truly the greatest sources of human wisdom, whether the Talmud was truly the highest level of knowledge and Truth."

Like so many Jews of this time, Yeshaya found himself caught between the familiar world of his childhood and the new one outside. Slowly but surely, he said, the "exciting and enchanting new universe" was winning out. "I felt a terrible emptiness inside. I yearned for the happiness I had known before…. I wanted to turn back the clock, but I could not."

This Ḥanukkah menorah was made in Russia at the end of the eighteenth century. Since the days of the Maccabees, every generation has faced the challenge of balancing the pull of the surrounding secular culture with the pull of their Jewish identities. Describe one thing you value about modern secular culture; one thing you value about Judaism.

Most Jews in Western Europe, though, had no interest in turning back the clock. They were more than willing to face the challenges of modern life. But they were concerned that the laws of emancipation and Jewish efforts at integration were not solving the problem of anti-Jewish prejudice. In fact, Jewish success seemed to stir up new resentment, providing more fuel for anti-Jewish feelings. Similarly, in Eastern Europe, hopes for a brighter future were dimmed. Alexander II was assassinated in March 1881. His death was blamed on the Jews and anti-Jewish riots broke out throughout the Pale.

Hannah Rachel Werbermacher

While some Jews chose to assimilate, others were more deeply drawn to Judaism. Hannah Rachel Werbermacher, known as the "Maid of Ludomir," was born in Poland in about 1805, a time when it was extraordinary—to some, even unacceptable—for a woman to become a Jewish scholar. Yet Werbermacher was determined to become learned, and she succeeded.

After her parents' deaths, Werbermacher established her own synagogue. It was called *die Grüne Schule* (the green synagogue). There she gave sermons on Shabbat to her Ḥasidic followers. She later immigrated to the Land of Israel, where she continued to study mysticism and worked to speed the coming of the Messiah.

then & NOW

Many supporters of the new "Reform Judaism" were inspired by the work of scholars who were associated with the Society for Jewish Culture and Science. These scholars had found that change over time was a constant feature of Judaism. The Reformers argued that they were restoring Judaism's original ethical spirit by shedding rabbinic innovations that had become meaningless in modern times.

Today, Judaism's ethical *mitzvot,* especially the pursuit of social justice, continue to be important in Reform Judaism. Yet, both the return to earlier traditions and the spirit of innovation also remain hallmarks of Reform Judaism. In the 1930's, the Reform movement officially reversed its opposition to Zionism, the commitment to establish and support a modern Jewish state in the Land of Israel.

Also, in recent years, many Reform congregations have increased their use of Hebrew and embraced the tradition of wearing *kippot* and *tallitot* during prayer services. As innovators, Reform Jews were the first to formally ordain female rabbis, beginning with Sally Priesand in 1972.

Each generation continues to adapt Judaism to the modern world. Interview your rabbi or cantor, or use the Internet or resources from your synagogue's library, to find one difference between the traditions of your synagogue and those of earlier congregations in your movement.

_____

_____

_____

_____

_____

Chapter 13 The Rise of Antisemitism

Nationalism and the Search for Scapegoats

investigate

- Why did some Europeans resent and mistrust the Jews?

- How did the Jews respond to anti-Jewish prejudice?

- What can Jewish history teach us about the prejudice we encounter against Jews and others?

Key Words and Places

Nationalism

Chauvinism

Scapegoat

Antisemitism

The BIG Picture

By the mid-nineteenth century, the Jews of Western and Central Europe were becoming less and less distinguishable from their non-Jewish neighbors. They spoke the same language, lived next door to one another, enjoyed the same music and literature, and wore the same fashions.

To Europeans who opposed Jewish equality and integration, this was cause for alarm. In the past, hatred of Jews was often based on religious differences, such as the Jews' rejection of Jesus as the Messiah. Now, it was expressed in ethnic terms, with attacks on the Jews as a nation rather than as a religious group. It also was expressed in racial terms, with claims that Jews were an intellectually and morally inferior race.

early 1800's	1869	1871
Industrial Revolution spreads from Britain to other Western European nations	**World History:** First U.S. professional baseball team, the Cincinnati Red Stockings, begins playing	Small German states form unified nation of Germany

"Us" and "Them"

In 1871, the many small German states came together, forming the unified nation of Germany. It was a time of growing **nationalism,** a strong feeling of loyalty and devotion to one's own nation over other groups. Unification made many Germans more conscious of the ties that bound them together: common language, culture, history, and land. Nationalists became less tolerant of those who did not share their ancestry, including Jews, because they were seen as a threat to German unity and national purity.

When national pride becomes extreme and inspires feelings of superiority, it turns into **chauvinism.** On the rise throughout Europe, nationalism encouraged people to think of the world in terms of *us and them.* When nationalism intensified into chauvinism, people began to question whether or not the Jews belonged. Were they truly French, German, Russian, Dutch? Or were they a nation within a nation?

late 1800's	1894	1897	1906
Antisemitism becomes common aspect of everyday life in much of Europe	Alfred Dreyfus, Jewish officer in French army, placed on trial	Antisemitic politician Karl Lueger elected mayor of Vienna, Austria	Dreyfus cleared of all charges

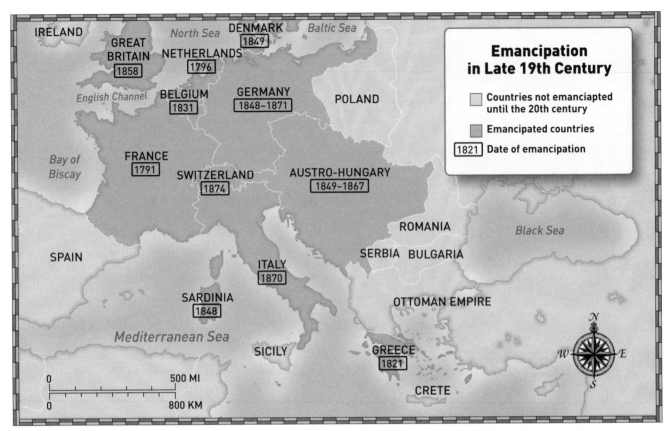

By 1871, most European countries had emancipated the Jews. Rapid Jewish assimilation and economic success in countries like France, Germany, and Austria sometimes stirred resentment that resulted in antisemitism.

Us and Them

GERMANS ("US")		JEWS ("THEM")
We speak German.	→	They speak German *and* Yiddish.
We live according to German traditions.	→	They have strange customs and holidays.
We have German ancestors.	→	They have Semitic ancestors.
We have allegiance to Germany alone.	→	They feel connected to the Land of Israel.

Searching for Scapegoats

The Industrial Revolution also brought great change. As jobs moved from farms to urban factories, people in rural areas uprooted their families in search of work. Families that had lived on farms for generations were now crowded into chaotic, polluted cities. Many found it hard to adjust. They felt as if their world and all they valued were being destroyed.

In difficult times, people can be tempted to look for a **scapegoat,** or someone to blame. In nineteenth-century Europe, Jews were a common scapegoat. Because so many Jews already lived in cities, they were associated with city life. Also, because they seemed to be doing well, enjoying middle-class jobs and lifestyles, they inspired envy in Europeans who were less successful in adapting to city life.

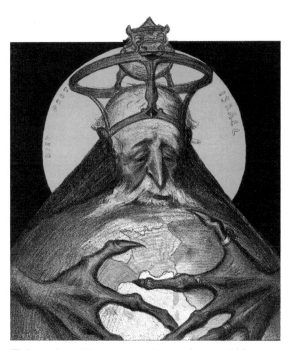

This antisemitic cartoon shows the world in the grasp of the Jews, as symbolized by James (Jacob) Rothschild, a leading member of a wealthy, international Jewish banking family.

A common complaint was that as the Jews were rising into the middle class, they were taking jobs from non-Jews. In reality, Jews made up a small percentage of the population and in all professions they were far outnumbered by successful non-Jews. But **antisemitism,** or prejudice against Jews, distorted the facts. It made the Jews scapegoats for the failures and problems of others. For some, it also made the Jews' relative success infuriating.

By the late 1800's, antisemitism was common in much of Europe. Right-wing politicians found they could win elections with openly antisemitic campaigns. In the Austrian capital of Vienna, for example, a violently antisemitic man named Dr. Karl Lueger was elected mayor. Throughout Germany, signs appeared barring Jews from the best hotels and restaurants. Antisemitic speech became acceptable in shops, classrooms, and government offices.

"Death to the Jews"

In November 1894, Captain Alfred Dreyfus, a Jewish artillery officer in the French army, was placed on trial for selling military secrets to the Germans. Throughout his trial, the antisemitic press warned of an "international Jewish conspiracy" and demanded that Dreyfus be convicted. Despite weak evidence, Dreyfus was found guilty.

After the trial, the military stripped Dreyfus of his rank at a humiliating public ceremony. "Soldiers!" he protested. "An innocent is dishonored." But his pleas were drowned out by the crowd's chants of "Death to Dreyfus! Death to the Jews!"

Some non-Jews spoke out in support of Dreyfus. *"J'Accuse!"* ("I Accuse!"), screamed the

The "Science" of Racism

The nineteenth century was dominated by great scientific advances. Sewage systems were installed in cities, vaccines were invented against many killer diseases, and doctors began sterilizing their instruments before operating on patients.

Impressed by the power of science to strengthen society, many people turned to science to justify their prejudices. In Philadelphia, a white doctor, Samuel Morton, announced that races could be ranked by the size of their brains. By measuring skulls of whites and blacks, he was able to "prove" that whites were superior.

Antisemites were obsessed with Jews' bodies, which they claimed were inferior to Indo-European, or Aryan, bodies. In books and cartoons they portrayed Jews with flat feet, hawk-shaped noses, thick lips, and dark complexions. Antisemites also charged that Jewish men could not measure up to the masculine ideal. They portrayed them as weak and nervous—the opposite of "real men." Today these stereotypes may be signs of ignorance, but at the time many people believed they were scientific truths.

Dreyfus in court. The Dreyfus Affair, as it is commonly known, divided France for over a decade. "Because he was a Jew he was arrested," wrote Bernard Lazare, one of Dreyfus's Jewish supporters. "Because he was a Jew he was convicted, because he was a Jew the voices of justice and truth could not be heard in his favor!"

headline of a passionate defense of Dreyfus. It was written by France's most popular author, Émile Zola. The open letter to the president of France was published on January 13, 1898. But antisemites were equally passionate. Antisemitic riots swept through many French cities and towns. As for Zola, he was forced to flee France.

In 1906 Dreyfus was finally cleared of all charges and allowed to resume his army career. But the lasting message of the Dreyfus Affair was not his eventual legal victory. It was that more than a century after the emancipation of French Jews, antisemitism was still a force in French social and political life.

Émile Zola's famous letter in defense of Dreyfus was printed on the front page of *L'Aurore*, a literary magazine.

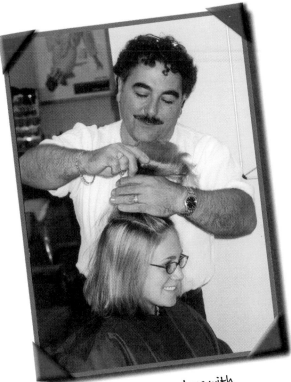

One way we treat ourselves with dignity is to take care of our personal appearance. But when does a healthy concern for how we look turn into an obsession? When do the ways in which we alter our bodies signal disrespect rather than respect for who we are?

The Plague of Self-Doubt

Jewish reactions to antisemitism varied. Some of the more assimilated Jews found their own scapegoats for antisemitism. They blamed newly immigrated Eastern European Jews, many of whom were streaming into Western and Central European cities during this period.

The East Europeans seemed to be the living image of the antisemitic stereotypes. They dressed differently and had not yet adopted middle-class values and lifestyles. Many still spoke with heavy accents or, even worse, spoke only Yiddish. In short, Western and Central European Jews were embarrassed by their Eastern European brothers and sisters.

Many Jews also started to doubt themselves. After hearing the anti-Jewish rants for so long,

Jacques Joseph

Jacques Joseph, son of a rabbi, was one of the most sought-after surgeons in Berlin in the early 1900's. A plastic surgeon, Dr. Joseph is considered by some to be the father of modern facial plastic surgery.

Dr. Joseph would not be of special interest, but for the fact that the majority of his patients were Jews. Most had inferiority complexes about their looks and came to Dr. Joseph for a "nose job." He boasted that by operating on their noses, he cured their heads—their emotional problems.

Surrounded by a racist culture that prized blond hair and small noses, many Jews looked in the mirror and felt contempt for their bodies. Do you think that Dr. Joseph helped or harmed such patients? Why?

_____

_____

_____

What sorts of ideal images of beauty does our society have? Are they prejudicial to some people? Explain your answer by giving examples.

_____

_____

_____

_____

they began to wonder: *Could there be some truth to what they are saying?* Some were so plagued by doubt that they were driven to self-hatred. Among the most notorious self-haters was the Jewish-born philosopher Karl Marx, who claimed, "Money is the jealous God of Israel and that God has become the Lord of the universe."

In Germany, many Jews tried to become more German than the Germans. They embraced the German idea of self-improvement through culture and education. Jewish men, in particular, tried to improve their body image by joining gymnastics associations. They tried to prove their masculinity by learning to duel. A scar on one's face made by the duelist's blade was considered a mark of honor. When cuts were made, they were treated in a way to ensure that a permanent scar remained.

Looking Ahead

Despite their experience with antisemitism, at the end of the nineteenth century many Jews were still optimistic about the future. They believed in progress and considered anti-semitism to be an ancient prejudice that would eventually die out. After all, many Central and Western European Jews were succeeding professionally and gaining the acceptance of non-Jewish neighbors.

Others were not convinced that Jews would ever be accepted as equals. Looking across the ocean, they saw hope for a better life in the United States. They wondered if it was worth

packing up everything they owned to sail across the Atlantic and start their lives over in a new world. For more and more European Jews, the answer was *yes.*

Karl Marx, who went on to write the *Communist Manifesto* with Freidrich Engels, accepted the antisemitic stereotype that all Jews were businesspeople.

Cross the Atlantic—
Yes or No?

Imagine that you are living in Europe at the end of the nineteenth century. Your family has experienced antisemitic attacks but you are hopeful that new professional and social opportunities soon will open up for you.

List two reasons to remain in Europe and two to set sail for North America.

Remain in Europe

1. _____

_____

2. _____

_____

Set Sail for North America

1. _____

_____

2. _____

_____

What is your final decision—to stay or to go? Why?

_____

_____

_____

Just as the Jews became scapegoats, so, too, other groups and individuals are sometimes made into scapegoats. When we shift responsibility for our own shortcomings and insecurities onto others, we make them into scapegoats. When people start to judge others as inferior or to spread rumors, it is a red flag to address their own weaknesses and fears.

1. Why might making someone into a scapegoat feel good at first?

_____

_____

2. Why can't making someone into a scapegoat solve a problem in the long term?

_____

_____

3. Everyone has both strengths and weaknesses. When someone notices a weakness of yours, what strengths do you hope they will also notice? Why?

_____

_____

4. When you notice other people's weaknesses or shortcomings, what is the benefit of also seeking their strengths?

_____

_____

Chapter 14 U.S. Jewry, 1820–1880

Balancing Freedom and Tradition

investigate

- What differences arose among American Jews?

- How did these differences challenge the community?

- How did the diversity of views and practices contribute to the development of an American style of Judaism?

- In what ways is diversity characteristic of Judaism in our country today?

Key Words and Places

Union of American Hebrew Congregations

Hebrew Union College

Pittsburgh Platform

Young Men's/ Women's Hebrew Association

Jewish Theological Seminary

The BIG Picture

In the mid-1800's, the United States experienced one of the greatest economic expansions in world history. Factories were booming in cities and a growing system of canals and railroads was revolutionizing travel and commerce. To keep the economy growing, the United States needed workers—it needed immigrants. Millions poured in from Ireland, Germany, China, and many other lands.

Among the new arrivals in search of a better life were thousands of European Jews, their journey fueled by Europe's rising wave of antisemitism. In the United States, Jews found the economic opportunities and freedom they had dreamed of. They also found new challenges that threatened the unity of the Jewish community.

1849	1851	1854	1860
Jewish "forty-niners" move west as part of California gold rush	Chicago has a synagogue, kosher butcher, and Jewish day school	First Young Men's Hebrew Association founded in Baltimore	Jewish population of United States reaches 150,000; over two hundred synagogues exist across United States

Seeking a Fresh Start

Abraham Kohn was one of about 150,000 Jewish immigrants who came to the United States from Germany, Lithuania, western Poland, and other parts of Central Europe between 1820 and 1880. He came from a small town in Germany and had little education. Facing a doubtful economic future and legal discrimination, he decided to take a chance and come to the United States. In the United States, he traveled the countryside as a peddler, until he had earned enough money to open a store in Chicago.

The High Cost of Earning a Living

Peddlers filled their packs with anything and everything they could carry and sell—dishes, sewing supplies, tools, and secondhand clothing. But the peddler's life was not an easy one and observing Jewish ritual and laws was often difficult. As Abraham Kohn's diary reveals, life in America challenged Jewish observance and unity.

> Thousands of peddlers roam about America—young, strong men wasting their strength by carrying heavy burdens in the heat of summer and losing their health in the freezing cold of winter. And so they entirely forget their Creator. They cease to put on their tefillin; they do not pray on work days nor on Shabbat. Indeed, they have given up their religion for the packs on their backs. Is such a life not enslavement rather than freedom?
> —Abraham Kohn, July 29, 1842

Imagine that you are a Jewish peddler in the mid-1800's. Why might observing Jewish tradition and ritual be a comfort to you?

_____

_____

Why might it feel like a burden?

_____

_____

How might you adapt Judaism to your new American way of life?

_____

_____

By the SUPREME EXECUTIVE COUNCIL of the Commonwealth of *Pennsylvania.*

WHEREAS *Solomon Raphael* the Bearer hereof, intending to follow the Business of a Pedlar within the Commonwealth of *Pennsylvania,* hath been recommended to Us as a proper Person for that Employment, and requesting a Licence for the same: WE DO hereby licence and allow the said *Solomon Raphael* to employ himself as a Pedlar, and Hawker within the said Commonwealth, to travel *with one Horse* to expose and vend divers goods & merchandize until the *twenty first* Day of *March* next; Provided he shall, during the said Term, observe and keep all Laws and Ordinances of the said Commonwealth to the same Employment relating.

GIVEN under the Seal of the Commonwealth, at Philadelphia, the *twenty third* Day of *March* in the Year of our LORD One Thousand Seven Hundred and *eighty seven*

ATTEST.

On March 23, 1787, Solomon Raphael received this license to be employed as a peddler in Pennsylvania.

From Peddler to Merchant

Many peddlers eventually succeeded in opening their own stores. The "Jew's Store" became a regular fixture on the main streets of small southern and western towns. Some Jews succeeded in building their businesses into department store chains that are household names today. These stores include Macy's, Bloomingdale's, and Neiman Marcus.

In New York, by 1880, Jews owned about 80 percent of all retail and 90 percent of all wholesale clothing firms. Outside New York, about 75 percent of all clothing firms were Jewish owned.

Peddlers like Kohn created new Jewish communities across the United States, from Portland, Maine, to Portland, Oregon. By 1851, for example, Chicago had a synagogue, kosher butcher, and Jewish day school. Some Jews remained traditionally observant. Others intermarried and shed their Judaism. Still others began to experiment with liberalizing Jewish laws and Americanizing Jewish worship. The result was that a uniquely American Jewish culture developed.

Jewish Forty-Niners Hit the Frontier

In 1849, everyone—including the Jews—was talking about the discovery of gold in California. Many Jewish "forty-niners" rushed west, hoping to scoop golden nuggets from the streams of California. Others saw a different opportunity, the chance to earn a living by supplying goods to the settlers, including the miners.

It was this dream that drew Levi Strauss, a Jewish immigrant peddler from Bavaria, to the West in 1853. Strauss was convinced that goods from the East would be in demand in San Francisco. He booked passage on a ship sailing from New York to San Francisco and brought merchandise with him. His ship was still anchored in the harbor when merchants rowed out and bought up most of his stock.

Soon Strauss himself was watching for arriving ships and rushing out to buy their

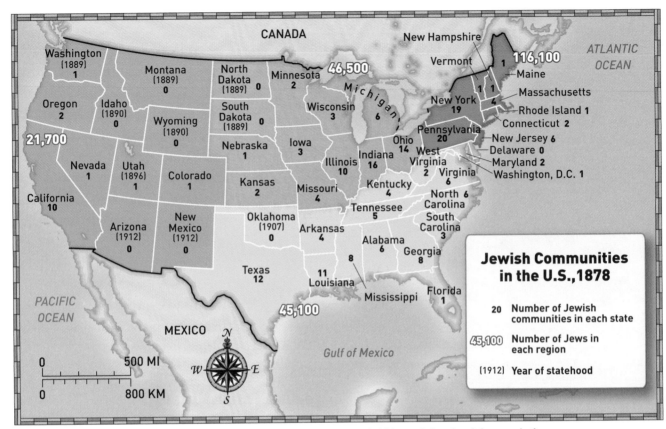

Jewish Communities in the U.S., 1878

20	Number of Jewish communities in each state
45,100	Number of Jews in each region
(1912)	Year of statehood

Map labels (states and values):

- Washington (1889) 1
- Oregon 2
- California 10
- 21,700
- Nevada 1
- Idaho (1890) 0
- Utah (1896) 1
- Arizona (1912) 0
- Montana (1889) 0
- Wyoming (1890) 0
- Colorado 1
- New Mexico (1912) 0
- North Dakota (1889) 0
- South Dakota (1889) 0
- Nebraska 1
- Kansas 2
- Oklahoma (1907) 0
- Texas 12
- 45,100
- Minnesota 2
- Iowa 3
- Missouri 4
- Arkansas 4
- Louisiana 11
- Wisconsin 3
- Illinois 10
- Michigan 6
- Indiana 16
- Mississippi 8
- Tennessee 5
- Alabama 6
- Kentucky 4
- Ohio 14
- West Virginia 2
- Georgia 8
- Florida 1
- 46,500
- New York 19
- Pennsylvania 20
- Virginia 6
- North Carolina 6
- South Carolina 3
- 116,100
- Vermont 1
- New Hampshire
- Maine 1
- Massachusetts 1
- Rhode Island 1
- Connecticut 2
- New Jersey 6
- Delaware 0
- Maryland 2
- Washington, D.C. 1
- CANADA
- MEXICO
- ATLANTIC OCEAN
- PACIFIC OCEAN
- Gulf of Mexico
- 0 — 500 MI
- 0 — 800 KM

By 1880, the population of the United States was just over 50,000,000, and the Jewish population was 250,000. According to the Canadian census of 1881, there were 2,443 Jews in Canada.

merchandise so that he could sell it in San Francisco. As his business grew, he began transporting goods by train to merchants in smaller mining towns. By the early 1870's Levi Strauss & Company was a thriving business and Strauss was a millionaire.

Strauss may have been the most famous pioneer Jew, but he was hardly alone. Lewis Franklin found that out in September 1849, when he placed an ad in a San Francisco newspaper inviting Jews to his small store for Rosh Hashanah services. Immigrants from England, Germany, Poland, and Australia were among the thirty Jews who showed up. Together they conducted what is believed to have been the first public Jewish religious service in the Far West. By 1851 there were enough Jews in San Francisco to form two congregations. By the 1870's, Jews had fanned out to towns throughout the West.

Synagogues Sprout Up

The Jewish population of the United States grew from under 5,000 in 1820 to about 150,000 in 1860. Many Jews settled in growing eastern cities such as New York and Philadelphia. Others helped build new Jewish communities across the United States. As Jewish immigrants settled in new cities and established businesses and families, they also built synagogues and communal organizations, such as B'nai B'rith. These institutions created a sense of unity and provided support, for example, in the observance of weddings, births, and burials.

Levi's Jeans

The story of Levi's jeans—an icon of American culture—dates back to the gold rush, when Levi Strauss began selling a French denim cloth called "genes." One of his customers was Jacob Davis, a Jewish tailor in Reno, Nevada. Davis made pants out of the cloth and sold them to miners.

When Davis received a complaint that the pockets were tearing, he strengthened the pants by putting metal rivets at the points of greatest stress. He wanted to patent his new invention, but didn't have the sixty-eight dollars required to file the papers. So Davis wrote to Strauss, suggesting that they become partners. "The secratt of them Pents is the Rivits," Davis wrote.

Strauss liked the idea and the two men became partners. On May 20, 1873, they received patent No. 139,121—and blue jeans were born.

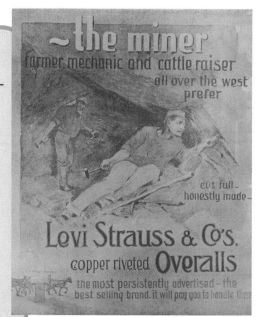

Levi Strauss used the theme of miners in this turn-of-the-century advertisement. In addition to being a successful business-man, Strauss was also active in the Jewish community and a member of San Francisco's Temple Emanu-El.

When George Washington was inaugurated as president in 1791, only six Jewish congregations existed in the United States, all on the eastern seaboard. By 1860 there were over two hundred congregations spread across the entire country. Some were small enough to meet in private homes. But in cities with large Jewish populations, such as San Francisco, New York, and Philadelphia, Jews often separated into two or more congregations, usually along ethnic lines.

One example of a split along ethnic lines took place in New York. Shearith Israel, established largely by Sephardic Jews sometime between 1695 and 1704, was the first Jewish congregation in North America. In 1825, the congregation split in two. B'nai Jeshurun, the new congregation, was led by Ashkenazic Jews. It distinguished itself from Shearith Israel through its Ashkenazic rituals and prayer book.

In 1818 Rebecca Gratz founded the Hebrew Sunday School Society of Philadelphia. It was radically different from other Jewish religious schools of its time. Girls and boys were taught together, classes were held only once a week, lessons were presented in English, not Hebrew, and all the teachers and administrators were women.

Civil War Strains Community

The tense years leading up to the Civil War severely strained the unity of American Jews. As might be expected, Jews usually held opinions similar to those of their neighbors. Southern Jews tended to support slavery, while northern Jews opposed slavery and the breakup of the Union. There were some exceptions, such as Rabbi David Einhorn of Baltimore, who was run out of town for his opposition to slavery.

When the fighting began in 1861, some Jewish families literally split in two. Four sons of the Jonas family in Illinois fought for the South, while a fifth took up arms for the North. Alfred Mordecai, a Jewish West Point graduate and a general in the Union army, sat out the war rather than fight against the Confederacy, where most of his family lived.

The most famous Jew on either side was Judah Benjamin, a U.S. senator from Louisiana who served in President Jefferson Davis's cabinet as attorney general, secretary of war, and finally secretary of state. A total of almost eight thousand Jews served in the Union and Confederate armies. And while the war divided American Jews, it also helped strengthen many Jews' ties to their adopted land.

Reform Judaism Evolves

The Reform movement gained strength with the arrival of religious leaders from Central Europe like Rabbi Isaac Mayer Wise. Wise was committed to Reform Judaism and a great believer in Jewish unity. He was willing to make compromises if he thought they could unite Jews.

Leading Congregation Beth El in Albany, New York, Wise broke with tradition by organizing a children's choir that included both boys and girls. He also admitted that he did not believe in the Messiah or in the rising to life of the dead at the End of Days. Shocked, Beth El's president fired him. Wise's supporters then established a new congregation in Albany called Anshe Emeth, meaning "people of truth."

In 1854, Wise moved to Ohio, where he led the Reform congregation Bene Yeshurun in

Ernestine Rose was known as "Queen of the Platforms." She spoke out publicly on the major social issues of her day, including the emancipation of slaves and the right of women to vote. In 1869, Rose helped found the Women's Suffrage Society, which worked for the rights of American women.

A Special Passover Seder

Camped with his regiment in the mountains of West Virginia, Union army soldier J.A. Joel decided to conduct a Passover seder. A friend from back home sent him matzah and a haggadah. Then Joel gathered twenty Jews from the 23rd Ohio Volunteer Regiment. "We obtained two kegs of cider," Joel recounted, "a lamb, several chickens, and some eggs." For bitter herbs, they collected wild weeds.

The seder went well until the men ate the weeds, which were more spicy than expected. Their mouths on fire, they gulped down the alcoholic cider. Joel reported, "We forgot the law authorizing us to drink only four cups, and the consequence was we drank up all the cider. Those who drank the more freely became excited, and one thought he was Moses, another Aaron, and one had the audacity to call himself Pharaoh."

After a brief interruption, the seder continued. "There, in the wild woods of West Virginia," Joel said, "away from home and friends, we consecrated and offered up to the ever-loving God of Israel our prayers and sacrifice."

If you could invite Joel to your seder, with what might he be *familiar*? With what might he be *unfamiliar*?

Familiar _____

Unfamiliar _____

Interview two of your classmates about their seders. Record two things that are the same at your seder and theirs, and two that are different.

Same	Different
1. _____	1. _____
_____	_____
2. _____	2. _____
_____	_____

Cincinnati. A year later, he published a Reform prayer book called *Minhag America* ("American Custom"), which deleted portions of the traditional prayer book that did not meet "the wants and demands of the time." For example, Wise deleted all references to the rebuilding of the ancient Temple.

Wise also inspired the creation of the first synagogue organization in 1873. Originally named the **Union of American Hebrew Congregations (UAHC),** it is now called the Union of Reform Judaism (URJ). Two years later, Wise opened the first successful rabbinical school, **Hebrew Union College (HUC),** in Cincinnati, where Reform rabbis, cantors, and educators are still trained today.

In 1885, Reform leaders held a meeting in Pittsburgh. There they adopted a radical platform, or set of policies, that cut many of their ties to halachah. Their reasoning was that a number of traditions, such as keeping kosher, lacked an ethical basis or were not meaningful to modern Jews. The Reform rabbis also declared that they no longer considered themselves part of a separate Jewish people or nation, but only part of the Jewish religion. This weakened their connection with the Land of Israel.

The **Pittsburgh Platform** did not represent the opinions of all Reform rabbis and was never officially adopted by the Reform movement. But it did strongly influence Reform Judaism in America for the next fifty years.

From Crisis to Strength

In spite of their accomplishments, the self-confidence of many American Jews gave way to a sense of crisis by the late nineteenth century.

For two hundred years, beginning in about 1650, American girls learned how to embroider by creating samplers, using silk thread on linen material. The girls often stitched the alphabet on their samplers. In this way, they not only learned to embroider but also learned their letters. By including the English and Hebrew alphabets, this sampler shows the desire of Jews to embrace both the American *and* Jewish traditions.

Antisemitism appeared to be on the rise. In one famous incident, a wealthy Jewish banker named Joseph Seligman was turned away at the Grand Union Hotel, a popular vacation spot in Saratoga Springs, New York. Jews were also disturbed by evangelical efforts to add an amendment to the Constitution making the

EUROPEAN JUDAISM	AMERICAN JUDAISM
Jewish communities in limited areas	Jewish communities spread out
Slow to change	More radical approach to change
History of legalized discrimination	History of freedom from oppression
Prayer books reflect the views and needs of European Jews	Prayer books reflect the views and needs of American Jews, including Jews from different European countries
Reform Judaism liberalized tradition	Reform Judaism liberalized tradition
Chief rabbis connected to the state	Separation of church and state; no chief rabbi

United States a Christian country. Finally, there was concern about rising rates of assimilation and intermarriage.

Some Jewish leaders responded by promoting a revival of Jewish learning and observance. They hoped to renew interest in Judaism and to strengthen Jewish self-confidence in the face of antisemitism. Like Reform Jews, they believed in adapting Judaism to American culture. But unlike the radical Reformers, the revivalists also emphasized how the Jews were different from their Christian neighbors.

Like the Reformers, the revivalists strengthened their movement through the creation of organizations and institutions, many of which still exist today. The first **Young Men's Hebrew Association (YMHA)** was founded back in 1854 in Baltimore. The name was adapted from the Young Men's Christian Association (YMCA). But while the YMCA's activities were mostly religious and athletic, the YMHA's programs were much broader. They included literary groups, lectures, orchestras, glee clubs, libraries, and sometimes employment bureaus. By 1890 there were 120 YMHAs across the country and by 1888 there were the beginnings of the **Young Women's Hebrew Association (YWHA)**.

In 1886, the **Jewish Theological Seminary (JTS)** was established. It sought to adapt Judaism to modern life while preserving in America "the knowledge and practice of historical Judaism." Eventually, JTS became the intellectual, spiritual, and educational center of Conservative Judaism. Today it trains Conservative rabbis, cantors, and educators.

Building a Jewish Future

In barely a generation, the Jews of the 1800's succeeded in building an American Jewish

Emma Lazarus

Emma Lazarus was one of the best-known participants in the revival movement. Born in 1849, her family traced its roots back to the first Jewish settlers in America in 1654. Lazarus sought to balance her American identity with pride in her Sephardic heritage and the commitment to help revitalize Jewish life in America.

Emma Lazarus wrote "The New Colossus" shortly before her death in 1887. Her poem helped create the vision of the United States as a safe haven for oppressed people.

Encouraged by her father, Lazarus began writing poetry as a teen. She is best known for her poem "The New Colossus," which is engraved on a bronze plaque at the base of the Statue of Liberty. It calls out in the name of America and liberty, "Give me your tired, your poor, your huddled masses yearning to breathe free...."

From 1882 to 1883, Lazarus wrote a series of open letters, "An Epistle to the Hebrews." In the letters she presented her views on how to reinvigorate Jewish life through a cultural and national revival in the United States and in the Land of Israel. Partly in response to the raging pogroms, or massacres of Jews, in Russia, she argued for the creation of a modern Jewish homeland in Israel (which was then called Palestine).

In contrast to the Reform leaders of her time, who focused on Judaism as a religious heritage, Lazarus focused on Judaism as a national and cultural heritage. How do you think the Reform leaders who met in Pittsburgh in 1885 would have responded to Lazarus's call for the creation of a modern Jewish homeland in Israel? Why?

_____

_____

This early seal of the Jewish Theological Seminary was designed by Victor Brenner in 1902. Brenner later became well-known for his design of the United States penny in 1909. The image on the JTS seal shows the burning bush from which, the Torah tells us, God spoke to Moses. It also quotes Exodus 3:2—"The bush was not consumed." The seal's message is that American Judaism will be kept strong through the Jewish learning and wide-ranging scholarship of JTS.

flexibility and diversity had historically been a source of strength rather than weakness. American Jews believed that they, too, would succeed in building an exciting Jewish future.

You have inherited their tradition of diversity and creativity. You have stood on the shoulders of those who came before you, viewed the past, and learned from it. Now it is your turn to help build the Jewish future and a better, stronger world.

May you go from strength to strength.

culture, a wide variety of Jewish institutions, and an American style of Judaism. America had lived up to its reputation as a land of opportunity.

The very ingredients that had made America inviting—the extraordinary degree of freedom and the enormous economic opportunity—also drew some Jews away from their religion. But most cherished the view of themselves as links in the chain of Jewish tradition that extended back more than three thousand years. They knew that Jews had always adapted to modern ideas and changing times by creating new ways to celebrate Jewish tradition and culture. This

We live on a diverse planet in which all people must work together to create a better world. As Jews, the choices we make not only contribute to that effort but also add new details to the story of our people.

Glossary

Academy House of study established in the town of Yavneh after the destruction of the Second Temple. In time, academies were also established in the Diaspora. It was here that scholars and the best students studied, debated, and passed Jewish teachings from one generation to the next.

Antisemitism Prejudice against Jews.

Ashkenaz Hebrew word meaning "Germany." In the Middle Ages, the term *Ashkenazim* referred to Jews living in Germany and northern France. Today, it refers to Jews whose families originated in Germany and Eastern Europe.

Baptism A Christian ritual based on a Jewish purification ritual of *mikveh*, which requires that a person dunk his or her entire body in water.

Beit Hamikdash (Holy Temple) The spiritual and religious center of Jewish life in ancient Israel; located in Jerusalem.

Black Death A plague that swept across Europe between 1348 and 1350. It was the deadliest epidemic the world had ever seen, killing twenty-five million people, or about one-third of all Europeans.

Conversos Spanish Jews whose lives were spared in the late 1300's when they converted to Christianity.

Crucifixion A Roman execution technique in which the condemned were hung on a cross.

Crusade A Christian holy war.

Crypto-Jews (Secret Jews) *Conversos*, or Jews forced to convert to Christianity in the late 1300's, who continued to practice Judaism in secret.

Diaspora Places Jews live outside of the Land of Israel.

Disputations Debates. In the thirteenth century, Church leaders challenged rabbis to a series of public disputations.

Emancipation Political freedom that enabled Jews to become full-fledged citizens of their countries with all the rights of other citizens.

Epistles Letters Paul, a follower of Jesus, wrote to help educate new converts to Christianity. The Epistles eventually became the earliest books to be included in the New Testament.

Excommunicated To be cut off from one's religious community, for example the Jewish community, and shunned by its members.

Exiled Forced to leave one's home or country.

Gemara An elaboration on the Mishnah that includes discussions of Jewish law, interpretations of the Bible, parables, stories, traditions, and folklore.

Geonim (singular, Gaon) Great scholars of Talmud. *Gaon* was the official title of the heads of the Babylonian academies of Pumbedita and Sura.

Golden Age of Spain Period from about 950 CE to 1150 CE in which Spain was a leading center of Jewish learning and culture.

Gospels Christian sacred writings based on sayings and stories about Jesus's life.

Halachah Jewish law.

Haskalah (Enlightenment) A philosophical movement embraced by eighteenth- and nineteenth-century European-Jewish intellectuals. It emphasized the creative powers of the human mind, scientific experimentation, and reasoning.

Hebrew Union College (HUC) The first successful rabbinical school in the United States. It is now called Hebrew Union College-Jewish Institute of Religion (HUC-JIR) and trains Reform rabbis, cantors, and educators.

Inquisition A court set up in 1233 by the Catholic Church to investigate people who disagreed with Church teachings and rulings.

Islam The religion founded by Muhammad. Followers of Islam are called Muslims.

Jewish-Christians Jews who accepted Christian teachings during the early years of Christianity's development.

Jewish Theological Seminary of America (JTS) The intellectual, spiritual, and educational center of Conservative Judaism. JTS trains Conservative rabbis, cantors, and educators.

Judges Chieftains who ruled over the early Israelite tribes. Judges were responsible for settling disputes and led their tribes in times of war.

Kabbalah Teachings of the Jewish mystics.

Kehillah Organized Jewish community. Eastern European Jews were legally required by the secular government to belong to the *kehillah*.

Koran The holy book of Islam.

Ladino A language that is a mixture of Turkish, Hebrew, and Spanish; it is the Sephardic equivalent of Yiddish.

Marranos An insulting Spanish word meaning "swine"; the name given to those Sephardic Jews who were suspected of being secret Jews.

Mishnah The oldest postbiblical collection of Jewish laws. The Mishnah is based on oral law, or legal rulings that were passed by word of mouth from one generation to the next.

Mishneh Torah The fourteen-volume summary of Jewish law written by Maimonides.

Moneylenders Businesspeople who lend money and charge interest on the loans.

Mosques Muslim houses of worship.

Muslims Followers of Islam.

New Testament Christian sacred writings; the Christian Bible includes the New Testament and the Old Testament.

Old Testament The Hebrew Bible, which contains the Five Books of Moses, the Prophets, and the Writings.

Prophets Israelite spiritual leaders who taught God's ethical teachings, sometimes sought to predict the future, and gave kings political advice.

Resurrected Raised from the dead.

Separation of Church and State The protection of religious belief and practice from government interference.

Sepharad Hebrew word meaning "Spain." The term *Sephardim* refers to Jews whose families originated in Spain or Portugal.

Septuagint The written Greek translation of the Torah.

Shtetls Yiddish word meaning "little towns."

Shulḥan Aruch A book that clearly describes how Jewish law should be practiced; published in 1565 by Rabbi Joseph Caro.

Sinat Ḥinam Senseless hatred. Jewish tradition teaches that the underlying cause of Jerusalem's destruction in 70 CE was Jewish disunity and *sinat ḥinam*, the Jews' senseless hatred of one another.

State-Sponsored Religion Government establishment of one or more religions as the official religion(s) of the country.

Synagogue Greek word meaning "congregation." Early synagogues were a combination of prayer house, Jewish community center, and guest house.

Talmud The Mishnah and Gemara combined. Two versions of the Talmud were compiled. The Palestinian Talmud contains the discussions that were conducted in the rabbinic centers of the Galilee; the Babylonian Talmud contains the discussions conducted in the rabbinic centers of Babylonia.

Tisha B'Av The ninth day of the month of Av, which falls in the summer; a day of mourning for the destruction of the Holy Temple in Jerusalem.

Yiddish A language that is a mixture of Hebrew, Aramaic, and German. Yiddish first developed in Germany and is the Ashkenazic equivalent of Ladino.

Zohar Basic textbook of the Kabbalah, written by Moses de Leon.

Index

Hebrew Union College (HUC), 154, 155, 162 (def.), 166

heder, 132, 133 (def.)

Heine, Heinrich, 136

Hellenism, 16, 17 (def.), 18–23, 26–27, 29, 73, 132

heretics, 62, 72 (def.), 94

Herod, 28, 30–31, 33, 35, 50

High Priest, 16, 21, 22, 23, 26, 29, 30, 33, 52

Hillel, 28, 32, 39, 44

Hirsch, Samson Raphael, 138–39

Holdheim, Samuel, 132, 137

Holocaust, 42, 60

Holy Land, 12, 86, 87, 89, 90

Holy Temple, 6, 8 (def.), 12, 44, 46, 63, 65, 162, 166

  First Temple, 6, 37

    destruction of, 7, 10, 11, 13, 62

  Second Temple, 6, 7, 13 (def.), 16, 17, 21–24, 26, 29, 30, 31, 34–35, 50, 64, 69, 71

    destruction of, 29, 37–38, 40, 41, 42, 43, 45, 48, 49, 50, 51, 52, 55, 57, 64, 72, 84, 107, 166, 167

I

Industrial Revolution, 144, 147

infidels, 86, 87 (def.)

Innocent III, Pope, 86, 94

Inquisition, 86, 94 (def.), 95, 98, 100, 102, 104, 108, 115, 166

Isaiah, 10

Islam, 62, 67 (def.), 68–69, 71–72, 76, 99, 107, 166, 167

Israel, 6, 7, 8 (def.), 9, 13, 64

  Land of, vi, 2, 14, 17, 18, 30–31, 34, 44, 48, 51, 56, 65, 66, 78, 105, 137, 138, 142, 143, 146, 162, 164, 166

  Kingdom of, 6, 7–8, 10

  State of, 20, 26, 39, 42, 72, 104

Israelites, 2–5, 6–8, 11, 126

J

Jacobson, Israel, 136–37

Jason (Joshua), 21–23

Jeremiah, 12, 13

Jerusalem, 6, 7, 8 (def.), 10, 13, 14, 16, 17, 21, 22, 23, 24, 29, 30, 31, 33, 35, 36–38, 39, 40, 41, 43, 46, 48, 52, 60, 63, 67, 68, 69, 86, 90, 138, 166, 167

Jesus, 50, 52–53, 54, 55, 57, 58, 59, 61, 68, 91, 93, 144, 166

Jewish-Christians, 50, 55 (def.), 166

Jewish identity, vi–vii, 6, 15, 16, 19, 40, 55, 69, 72, 85, 108, 118, 122, 131, 141, 142

Jewish mystics, 74, 78 (def.), 79, 84, 167. *See also* mysticism.

Jewish Theological Seminary (JTS), 154, 155, 163 (def.), 165, 167

Jews, oppression of, vii, 48, 55, 58, 59, 84, 86–91, 93–96, 99–102, 103, 105, 108, 110–12, 122, 164. *See also* anti-semitism.

Joel, J. A., 161

John the Baptist, 50, 51–52, 59, 68

Joseph, Jacques, 150

Josephus Flavius, 35–36

Judah, 6, 8 (def.), 9–10, 13, 14, 17

Judah Maccabee, 24–25

Judah the Galilean, 28, 33–34

Judah the Prince, 63, 64, 65

Judaism

  adaptations of, 6, 15, 19–23, 26–27, 43–44, 46, 48, 49, 62, 63, 64, 68–69, 70, 71, 72, 73, 74, 77, 80, 84, 90, 93, 98, 108, 117, 120, 134–43, 163

  biblical, 62, 65 (def.)

  rabbinical, 62, 65 (def.), 66

Judea, 16, 17 (def.), 28, 62, 74

  divisions within, 21–23, 26–27, 28–30, 34–38, 43

  independence of, 24–26

  under Greek rule, 18–24, 132

  under Roman rule, 30–38, 40–48, 50–53

judges, 6, 7 (def.), 8, 167

K

Kabbalah, 74, 75, 78 (def.), 79, 105, 106, 167

kahal, 74, 82 (def.)

Kant, Immanuel, 118, 120

Karaites, 62, 71 (def.), 72

kehillah, 110, 111 (def.), 140, 167

Kohn, Abraham, 155–57

Koran, 62, 67 (def.), 68, 76, 167

L

Ladino, 98, 104 (def.), 167

Land of Canaan, 2, 4, 6

Lazarus, Emma, 164

Lithuania, Jews in, 96, 110, 111, 115–18

Lueger, Karl, 145, 147

Luria, Isaac, 99, 105, 109

M

Maccabees, 16, 24 (def.), 26, 46, 142

Maimonides, Moses, 75, 79, 80, 106, 167

marranos, 98, 100 (def.), 167

Masada, 28, 29, 33 (def.), 35, 38

maskilim, 118 (def), 120, 121, 140, 141

Mattathias, 24, 26

Menahem, 35

Mendelssohn, Moses, 119

Menelaus, 16, 22–23, 26

Messiah, 28, 33 (def.), 35, 46, 51, 52, 53, 57, 59, 99, 105, 106–7, 109, 115, 137, 138, 142, 144, 160

Middle Ages, 86, 91 (def.), 93, 166

mikveh, 51 (def.), 166

Minna of Worms, 89

Mishnah, 62, 63 (def.), 64, 71, 106, 166, 167

Mishneh Torah, 75, 79 (def.), 106, 167

Mitnagdim, 110, 118 (def.), 120, 121

moneylenders, 74, 79 (def.), 81, 89, 91–93, 133, 167

monotheism, 4, 54, 67, 68

Montefiore, Moses, 132, 135

Mordecai, Alfred, 160

Moses ben Nahman, 90

Moskowitz, Belle, 77

mosques, 62, 68 (def.), 72, 167

Muhammad, 62, 67, 68, 69, 166

Muslims, 62, 67 (def.), 68–69, 71–72, 74, 75, 77, 78, 81, 83, 84, 86, 87, 88, 89, 90, 99, 102, 166, 167

mysticism, 99, 105, 116, 142. *See also* Jewish mystics.

N

nagid, 74, 77 (def.)

Nasi, Doña Gracia, 103

nationalism, 144, 145 (def.)

Nebuchadnezzar, 9–10

Nehemiah, 7, 14

New Testament, 50, 54 (def.), 166, 167

O

Old Testament, 50, 54 (def.), 167

Onias, 21, 23

oral law, 62, 63 (def.), 71, 167

Orthodox Judaism, 121, 132, 135 (def.), 139